EMU 2000?

CHATHAM HOUSE PAPERS

A European Programme Publication

The Royal Institute of International Affairs, at Chatham House in London, has provided an impartial forum for discussion and debate on current international issues for 75 years. Its resident research fellows, specialized information resources, and range of publications, conferences, and meetings span the fields of international politics, economics, and security. The Institute is independent of government.

Chatham House Papers are short monographs on current policy problems which have been commissioned by the RIIA. In preparing the papers, authors are advised by a study group of experts convened by the RIIA, and publication of a paper indicates that the Institute regards it as an authoritative contribution to the public debate. The Institute does not, however, hold opinions of its own; the views expressed in this publication are the responsibility of the author.

CHATHAM HOUSE PAPERS

Simon ....
Univ. of
Manchester
Nov 1995

EMU 2000?

Prospects for European Monetary Union

Christopher Taylor

THE ROYAL INSTITUTE
OF INTERNATIONAL
AFFAIRS

Pinter
A Cassell Imprint
Wellington House, 125 Strand, London WC2R 0BB, United Kingdom

First published in 1995

British Library Cataloguing in Publication Data
A CIP catalogue record for this book is available from the British Library

ISBN 1-85567-313-4 (Paperback)
     1-85567-312-6 (Hardback)

Typeset by Koinonia Limited
Printed and bound in Great Britain by
Biddles Limited, Guildford and King's Lynn

Contents

Contents

Tables

Figures

Preface

The idea of writing this study developed a few years ago when I was working as an economist at the Bank of England, around the time of the Intergovernmental Conference on EMU and its aftermath. I was conscious then of a considerable unsatisfied demand among colleagues for a reliable guide to the burgeoning economic literature and empirical research on EMU, and for an objective analysis of the pros and cons of UK participation. When I left the Bank in 1994 to return to more academic work, I set myself to produce such a guide and this Chatham House Paper is the result.

I hope that the book will appeal to broadly three groups of readers. Firstly, it is designed to help busy policy-makers and officials who have some general economics background and who need to be conversant with all the main aspects of EMU, but who do not have the time to tackle the sources themselves. Secondly, I hope it will be of value to thinking people in business or public life who are interested in EMU because they realize that it is one of the great issues facing Europe and this country, and wish to be in a position to understand and contribute to the debate. Thirdly, I hope it will be of use to teachers and students in universities and sixth forms who are looking for a comprehensive but balanced and accessible account of EMU, perhaps for incorporation in a course on international monetary economics. Given the breadth of the prospective audience, I have tried to make the text readable for non-economists, while including enough technical argument and reference material to carry conviction with the more specialist reader.

As usual in such undertakings, the project would not have seen the light of day without a good deal of help from others. Above all, I am grateful to the Royal Institute of International Affairs for giving me a research home over the past nine months, and in particular to Susie Symes, former Head of the European Programme, and Jack Spence, Director of Studies, for their generous support and encouragement. Two discussion meetings were held in Chatham House, involving EMU specialists from the academic and business worlds, as well as the EC Commission, the European Monetary Institute, HM Treasury and the Bank of England, from many of whom useful feedback on earlier drafts was received. I acknowledge specially helpful comments from John Arrowsmith, Christopher Johnson and Charles Goodhart, all of whom read parts of the preliminary text with care beyond the call of duty.

I am pleased to acknowledge a particular intellectual debt to Peter Kenen, whose views on EMU have long influenced my own. Our contact over EMU dates from the time when he visited the Bank of England as Houblon-Norman Fellow in 1991, during the pre-Maastricht negotiations, in which he fortunately became deeply interested. As may be obvious from my text, I have had the great advantage of seeing the manuscript of his recent major study, published by Cambridge University Press, before finishing this work, although my first six chapters were already in draft and the remainder mapped out before I did so. I am also grateful to him for reading my complete manuscript and making many constructive points on it. Needless to say, all remaining errors and infelicities are mine entirely.

I also gratefully acknowledge patient help in locating difficult sources from Howard Picton at the Bank of England library and from the librarians at Chatham House; and assistance from Abigail Dennis on tables and charts, and many organizational matters. Finally my thanks are due to the staff of the Publications Department at Chatham House for their highly professional work on the final text.

August 1995 C.T.T.

Chapter 1

Introduction

Within the next few years the European Union will face momentous decisions which could greatly affect its economic and political development, perhaps permanently. The Member States are committed under the Maastricht Treaty to forming an economic and monetary union (EMU) by the end of the century. This would mean locking their exchange rates together permanently, with the aim of merging them into a single currency as soon as possible. Credibility and permanence would be achieved by pooling monetary sovereignty in a new European Central Bank (ECB), constituted with the full legal force of the Treaty. Not all Member States would join immediately, and a few might never do so. But the intention is to introduce a single money, in effect if not initially in form, throughout much of the Community by around the year 2000.

It is nevertheless not absolutely certain that EMU will go ahead then. Finance ministers, meeting in June 1995, have informally ruled out the possibility of the earlier start offered in the Treaty. Recurrence of currency turbulence in the spring of 1995 has had some effect in delaying the process, although it will probably not derail it completely; indeed by making the elimination of EC exchange rates seem more desirable, it may strengthen it. More basically, Germany's participation in EMU will be crucial, both economically and politically. Germany is the largest economy, has the best inflation record, and is generally perceived to have in the Deutschmark the most successful currency. Those who see EMU as a means to closer political integration would think it pointless to proceed without Germany. Although Germany is committed by the Treaty to joining, it could not be compelled to do so: ways could be found of postponing the project if the Germans are overtaken by doubts. However, a long delay seems unlikely because much political capital has been

1

invested in EMU and if it were shelved the damage to Community cohesion could be great. But the arguments about going ahead are by no means resolved, and decisions on EMU in Germany and elsewhere may be affected by the outcome of the Intergovernmental Conference (IGC) on political aspects of Union due to start in 1996. The issues addressed in this paper are therefore still very much in the balance, not least in the United Kingdom, whose decision on participation could arise initially in 1997.

There are two distinct views about the basic purpose of EMU. Some observers see it as an essentially economic development which would enable the full exploitation of the Single Market. On this view, the central question is whether EMU offers substantial economic benefits. Opinions differ on how far EMU implies a political dimension, but the economic issues are still paramount. Others see EMU as primarily a political phenomenon, not an end in itself. On this view, a single currency is more than just a symbol; it is the 'cornerstone of political union', according to leading German politicians (Schäuble and Lamers 1994). For them, the political issues are crucial.

This study does not take sides on that argument, but it is relevant to both. EMU may have important economic effects, whether or not they drive the project. Anyone who cares deeply about Europe's future must take them into account, and consider how the Maastricht design for EMU affects them. This paper is mainly about those economic questions, but it is not sensible to conduct the discussion in a political vacuum. The balance of economic effects proves to be highly uncertain, and cannot be resolved without introducing 'political economy' judgments.

Structure of the book

The next two chapters deal with background. Chapter 2 gives a brief guide to the Maastricht Treaty; it glosses over much detail, some of which will be elaborated later. Chapter 3 offers a short history of European monetary integration before EMU and explains why the Community is unlikely to be diverted from it.

The following three chapters discuss the economics of EMU, drawing on the academic literature. Chapter 4 summarizes the theory of optimal currency areas from its beginnings in the 1960s to later developments which stressed monetary policy. It identifies the main economic characteristics necessary for a successful currency area and assesses how far these are present in the Community, in the light of the empirical evidence.

Chapters 5 and 6 review the principal economic arguments for and against EMU, using as a framework the Commission's major study done in preparation for the EMU IGC. Chapter 5 concludes that there are likely to be long-term benefits for the Community as a whole, principally greater price stability, lower interest rates and savings in currency-conversion costs. Chapter 6 discusses the costs of abandoning the exchange-rate and national monetary policy as adjustment mechanisms. These are probably manageable in the 'core' States, given judicious use of other policies, but some non-core States suffer from structural problems for which exchange-rate adjustment provides an important if imperfect remedy; its absence in EMU could make their survival painful without a major expansion of transfer payments. The balance of effects is thus very uncertain and varies between different economies.

The rest of the study turns to the future of EMU and goes further into political economy issues. Chapter 7 describes key aspects of Stage II (the transition to full monetary union), now under way: the convergence criteria and which States are likely to meet them, drawing on Commission forecasts. It also discusses the contributions of the European Monetary Institute and the existing (basket) European Currency Unit (ECU) to the transition process. Chapter 8 examines key institutional features of Stage III – the conversion to the single currency, the role of the ECB, and the conduct of the single monetary policy. Major concerns are the ECB's weak accountability, and the potential conflict created by the separation of monetary and fiscal policy. Some remedies for what are seen as defects in the blueprint are offered.

Chapter 9 addresses the forthcoming decisions on EMU. It seeks to answer two main questions: whether the Community would be wise to form Stage III on Maastricht lines, and which countries should join. Particular attention is paid to how the United Kingdom should exercise the option it negotiated at Maastricht. This entails discussing alternative arrangements for non-participants, and prospects for the 1996 IGC. Consideration is also given to modifying certain features of Stage III; and to whether EMU will inevitably lead to political integration in time.

Chapter 2

The Maastricht Treaty

The Maastricht Treaty was agreed by the European Council (heads of State and government of the 12 Member States) in December 1991, after a year of intensive political negotiation (Council of the European Communities 1992).[1] It came into force on 1 November 1993, rather later than envisaged, ratification having met with delays and difficulties in several States.

Its full title is the 'Treaty on European Union'. 'European Union' is the umbrella term introduced at Maastricht to refer to the 'three-pillar' construction embracing the European Community and the two new areas of cooperation established in the Treaty – common foreign and security policy, which includes defence; and justice and home affairs, which covers mainly cooperation on crime, terrorism and immigration. The Treaty essentially comprises additions and amendments to the Treaty of Rome, which set up the European Economic Community in 1957.

The EMU provisions are the most explicit and definitive of the changes made. The other two pillars leave a lot of basic questions unresolved, and it was agreed at Maastricht to hold another IGC in 1996 to tackle the political issues. That conference could lead to further significant amendments to the Rome Treaty.

Key elements of Stage III

The Treaty's EMU provisions provide the legal basis for eventual full monetary union in the EC, and for the transition towards it. Full EMU, or 'Stage III' of the three-stage process envisaged in the Delors Report (Committee for the Study of Economic and Monetary Union 1989), will involve merging participating States' currencies into a single currency,

4

with a new central monetary institution, the European Central Bank, to issue and manage it. The ECB will formulate the single monetary policy required by EMU and administer it at the head of a European System of Central Banks (ESCB), of which participating States' central banks will be members. The constitution ('Statute') of the ECB and ESCB comprises one of some 18 protocols to the Treaty, and thereby has its legal force. Key features are the *mandate* given to the ECB to maintain price stability, to which it must give precedence over other economic objectives (*Statute*, Article 2);[2] its guarantee of *independence* from political interference (Article 7); and arrangements for *accountability* to EC institutions and the wider public (Article 15).

The ECB will perform many of the functions of a modern central bank: it will control the issue of all money and intervene in the markets to set key short-term interest rates throughout the system, hold and manage participating States' foreign exchange reserves and promote the smooth operation of payments systems. It may supply liquidity to the banking system, subject to the availability of 'adequate collateral' (*Statute*, Article 18). However, it will not be permitted to lend to governments except through the acquisition of their paper in the secondary markets (*Statute*, Article 21 and *Treaty*, Article 104);[3] and, although it may advise on prudential supervision of banks and on the stability of the financial system, it will not *undertake* supervision unless the Ministers' Council gives it a specific task at some future time (*Statute*, Article 25). The ESCB's federal structure will resemble somewhat that of the Deutsche Bundesbank, although the exact division of labour between the ECB and national central banks has yet to be decided.

The Treaty forbids certain financial practices thought inimical to EMU, namely 'excessive' government budget deficits (*Treaty*, Article 104c and 'Protocol on the excessive deficit procedure'); the 'monetary financing' of member governments by the ESCB (*Treaty*, Articles 104 and 104a); and the 'bailing out' of indebted member governments by EC governments or institutions (Article 104b). If the Economic and Finance Ministers' Council (ECOFIN) finds that a Member State's fiscal policy is grossly in error, there is provision in Stage III for sanctions, including the imposition of fines (Article 104c.11–13).

The president and directors who will run the ECB from day to day will be appointed by common accord of the European Council, on a recommendation from ECOFIN, but they and the central bank governors, who will together comprise the ECB's Governing Council, will be solely responsible for monetary policy. They will be hard to dismiss, and

ECOFIN will have no power to overrule them in their area of competence. The ECB will also manage the union's external exchange rate, but ECOFIN will decide exchange-rate *strategy*, although in doing so it must consult the ECB and respect the objective of price stability (*Treaty*, Articles 109.1 and 2).

ECOFIN will continue to exercise surveillance over other economic policies, which will remain a national responsibility. Each year ECOFIN must draft and, after discussion by the European Council, recommend the 'broad guidelines of the economic policies of the member States and of the Community' (*Treaty*, Article 103), and monitor developments in the Member States on the basis of reports by the Commission.[4] This strengthens somewhat the surveillance previously conducted at Community level, but the guidelines remain indicative. Where ECOFIN finds that economic policies are inconsistent with the guidelines or risk jeopardizing EMU it may make specific recommendations to the State concerned, and publish them, but the latter need not accept them, except in the area of fiscal deficits, which will be subject to the excessive-deficit procedure.

Key elements of Stage II

The Treaty also provides for *transition* to EMU – Stage II of the Delors process (*Treaty*, Chapter 4). The essential purpose of transition is to secure convergence of economic performance among EC States, with a view to preparing them for EMU. The key institutional innovation is the conversion of the pre-existing Committee of EC Central Bank Governors into the European Monetary Institute (EMI), intended as the forerunner of the ECB. The EMI has two main tasks: to strengthen the coordination of Member States' national monetary policies, though in this respect its function is advisory only, as monetary policy remains a national responsibility throughout Stage II; and to make the technical preparations for Stage III (*Treaty*, 'Protocol on the Statute of the European Monetary Institute', Articles 2–5).[5] This entails planning the instruments and procedures to be used by the ESCB, although their adoption will have to await the establishment of the ECB unless national monetary authorities choose to introduce them earlier.

The EMI has a number of subsidiary tasks, including the routine running of the EMS; overseeing the development of the ECU, which exists in the financial markets as a specialized asset mainly used by banks and financial institutions, but which is intended eventually to be the denominator of the single currency; and promotion of the efficiency of cross-border payments systems, an important element in the successful functioning of EMU. These two latter tasks are advisory only. There is also provision for the EMI to manage foreign-exchange reserves on behalf of Member States, but they are not obliged to use this facility.

The EMI duly came into existence on 1 January 1994 when Stage II started, and is now functioning. By then the ERM had not been consolidated as envisaged, with the lira and sterling suspended from the mechanism and the narrow band in abeyance; but freedom for capital movements between Member States had been almost completely established, and much of the legislation needed to create the Single Market in financial services had been agreed, if not fully implemented. In almost its last act before the Treaty came into effect, the European Council decided that the new body would be located in Frankfurt and it moved there in November 1994 from its temporary home in Basle. The Council expects that the ECB will also be located in Frankfurt if and when it takes over from the EMI. When Stage III starts, the EMI's functions in relation to non-participants in EMU will be assumed by the *General* Council of the ECB, whose membership will include all EU central bank governors.

Start of Stage III

The provisions relating to the start of Stage III are among the most complex and least clear in the Treaty. At the starting date, ECOFIN will fix participants' exchange rates irrevocably, including the rate at which 'the ECU shall be substituted for these currencies', a measure which 'by itself shall not modify the external value of the ECU', which implies that the fixing will be at or close to prevailing market rates (*Treaty*, Article 1091.4).[6] At that moment 'the ECU will become a currency in its own right', but no amplification is offered of this cryptic statement and the time interval between fixing rates and switching to the single currency is left open, except that it is to be 'rapid'.

The timing of the start of Stage III is also left uncertain. There is provision for the start to be before 1999, if a *majority* of Member States (8 out of 15, since the recent enlargement) meet the convergence criteria (*Treaty*, Article 109j.3). The first decisions on that are due to be made by the Council (at the level of heads of State or government, acting by qualified majority on the basis of a recommendation from ECOFIN), not later than 31 December 1996. ECOFIN has, however, already informally concluded (June 1995) that the convergence so far achieved will be insufficient to permit an early start, and that view was endorsed by the European Council at Cannes, although formal decisions have yet to be made. The Treaty provides that if no date has been set by the end of 1997, Stage III *must* start, with whichever States are judged eligible, on 1 January 1999 (*Treaty*, Article 109j.4). Formally, therefore, the Treaty leaves little alternative to starting EMU by 1999 at the latest. The only legal ground for delay beyond that would be either that no Member State is judged eligible, which seems unlikely, if only because of the 'relative' nature of most of the criteria (see below); or that a later date is set before the end of 1997, which is not inconceivable but would require a (qualified) majority vote. Although it seems unlikely now that a majority would support delay beyond 1999, they might do so if Germany or France really insisted.

The convergence criteria

The convergence criteria relate mainly to four aspects of national economic performance: inflation, the budget deficit, long-term interest rates, and 'observance of the normal fluctuation margins' of the ERM (*Treaty*, Article 109j.1 and 'Protocol on the convergence criteria'). They have been the subject of much attention and some criticism, as will be seen in Chapter 7. To be eligible for Stage III, an economy must have achieved a high degree of inflation convergence, fiscal balance and exchange-rate stability, and these achievements must be durable, as reflected in interest differentials. The criteria are not intended to be applied mechanically; judgments will be made by ECOFIN and the European Council on the basis of recommendations from the Commission and the EMI, and after consulting the European Parliament (*Treaty*, Article 109j.2 and 3).[7]

Eligibility will also require compatibility of national legislation with Treaty provisions. In particular, there will be an examination to see that the legal status of the national central bank accords with the independence provisions, which is a requirement for participation in Stage III (*Treaty*, Article 108).

Opt-outs and derogations

In ratifying the Treaty, most Member States formally committed themselves to moving to EMU on the above lines, but there were two exceptions. The United Kingdom reserved the right to decide nearer the time, and this is set out in a separate protocol. Denmark also reserved the right not to move automatically to Stage III, and this is set out in another protocol. Subsequently, Denmark decided as a result of its first referendum on the Treaty (in 1992) that it would not join Stage III or adopt certain other aspects of the Treaty (for example, common defence policy), and this was subsequently recognized in a declaration by the European Council. On that understanding, Denmark ratified the Treaty after a second referendum.

Member States which are not found eligible receive a 'derogation', which means that they are exempted temporarily from the rights and obligations connected with membership of the ESCB, and from financial penalties under the excessive-deficit procedure (*Treaty*, Article 109k). However they must be re-examined under the convergence criteria at least once every two years – or earlier if a State wishes – and join EMU if found eligible.

Chapter 3

The road to Maastricht

Forerunners of monetary union

Maastricht was a landmark on a road which the Community has travelled for over 30 years, but which had much earlier antecedents. The first manifestation of serious intent in Europe – or indeed anywhere, according to some monetary historians – to regulate exchange rates appears to have been the Latin Monetary Union, which was formed in 1865 as a venture in monetary cooperation among France, Italy, Belgium and Switzerland, later joined by several others including Greece and Spain.[1] At the time, these countries maintained a bimetallic (gold-silver) standard for their currencies, which they sought to promote in competition with the gold standard, dominated by Britain (Papadia and Saccomanni 1994). The LMU was dominated by France, which intended it to be a counterweight to the growing economic power of Prussia as well as to the rising Sterling Area (Dyson 1994). It ceased to exist when its members abandoned bimetallism in favour of gold in 1878, but it was a forerunner of EMU in some respects: it was treaty-based, and it tried to grapple with the problem of multiple monies in an economically integrating group of countries (Papadia and Saccomanni, 1994, p. 60). However, while seeking to link participants' currencies to the French monetary system, it lacked a central institution and a single monetary policy.

European moves towards monetary integration were effectively superseded by the gold standard when it was in its ascendancy in the 35 or so years before the First World War. The gold standard did not amount to monetary union but there were strong parallels.[2] A common standard of value was provided by a single commodity, gold, and although there was no central monetary institution, participants tended to follow the Bank of England's policy lead; moreover, although there was no formal

10

international agreement, much less a treaty, participants normally observed certain unwritten rules. Participating central banks fixed their monetary units in terms of gold, there was free trade in gold, and citizens could usually buy or sell unlimited amounts of their national currency against gold at their central banks at close to the declared price. To the extent that these rules were observed, the system offered fixed exchange rates and imposed a fairly uniform monetary discipline on participants. Twelve countries, including all the most industrially advanced of the time, adhered to the standard from around 1880 to 1914,[3] and another 10 or more adopted it for part of the period. Its long survival as a fixed-rate system for its main members (the 'Club') appears to have been due less to pursuit of mechanical deflationary/inflationary disciplines, as commonly supposed, than to large flows of long-term investment and migration of labour between economies at different stages of industrial development (Panic 1992, Chapters 2 and 3).

The relative success of the classical gold standard in promoting stable prices, free trade and economic prosperity among its members until 1914 impressed European governments and most of them strove to return to gold after the war (Papadia and Saccomanni 1994, p. 61). But international economic conditions were different then, and efforts to revive the standard came to grief in the early 1930s. Even so, despite the Depression, the floating of sterling and the dollar, and competitive devaluations of their currencies, continental governments never gave up their interest in stable exchange rates, as witnessed by several international monetary conferences between the wars. And allegiance to fixed rates among Francophone and Latin countries has persisted since.

The campaign to stabilize exchange rates crossed the Atlantic during the Second World War and led to the Bretton Woods conference in 1944 and the establishment two years later of the Bretton Woods system. The novel features of that system were the elaborate code of rules operated by the International Monetary Fund; adjustability of par rates to meet fundamental disequilibria, subject to IMF permission; and balance-of-payments assistance, subject to IMF 'conditionality'. Such was the ascendancy of US trade and aid after the war that most industrial countries, including all the west Europeans, and in due course many developing countries, joined the system, and postwar monetary cooperation became truly global. For more than 20 years the Bretton Woods system of 'pegged-but-adjustable' rates promoted exchange-rate stability, currency convertibility, and a progressive freeing of trade and payments. Its perceived success until the late 1960s further interrupted the momentum of European monetary integration.

A different precursor of EMU did, however, emerge postwar in the European Payments Union, a response to the problem of inconvertibility of west European currencies then and the bilateral trading agreements inherited from the 1930s. The EPU was an international clearing system for the multilateral netting of trade payments, based initially on liquidity provided by US aid under the Marshall Plan. It was wound up in 1958 when its members were able to introduce convertibility for current-account transactions under IMF rules. It left not only a legacy of cooperation and consultation on settlement of international payments between European (and other) central banks at the Bank for International Settlements in Basle, but also an example of multilateral policy surveillance when Germany was in excessive deficit to the EPU in 1951 (Papadia and Saccomani 1994, p. 61). Some economists believe that the EPU could have developed into a useful European policy forum had it survived (Gros and Thygesen 1992).

The fact that formal economic integration in Europe began in the heyday of Bretton Woods helps to explain the dearth of references to monetary integration in the Community's founding treaties, although dissension between France and Germany about the best approach to monetary cooperation in the formative years was also a factor (Dyson 1994, p. 66). Neither the treaty setting up the European Coal and Steel Community in 1952 nor the Rome Treaty mentioned the exchange-rate regime specifically. Nevertheless in providing for coordination of economic policies the Rome Treaty (Article 107) did state that EEC members should regard their exchange-rate policies as 'a matter of common concern', and that rubric has survived as a basis for exchange-rate cooperation. In what was in some respects a precedent for the later EC currency 'snake' (see below), ex-members of the EPU agreed in the European Monetary Agreement (1960) to restrict movements in their exchange rates to ± 0.75% of their par values – less than the ± 2% allowed for European cross-rates under IMF rules. Jean Monnet's Action Committee for a United States of Europe in 1961 advocated a European Monetary Reserve System as a step towards a single currency and monetary policy. And the Commission's Action Programme of 1962 called for a 'second stage' of integration post-1970, which would include fixed exchange rates. The setting up of the EC Central Bank Governors' Committee by Council Decision in 1964 was intended to promote exchange-rate stability through closer coordination of national monetary policies.

The Werner Report

The true launching of the modern EMU process, however, probably dates from the Hague Conference of heads of State and government in December 1969. This conference discussed a timetable for EMU, based on Commission papers (known as the first Barre plan after the Commission's Vice-President Raymond Barre) and on a 'Plan for Action' devised by Pierre Werner, then Prime Minister and Finance Minister of Luxembourg. The Werner Committee was set up in March 1970 and the Council adopted Commission proposals (the second Barre plan) based on its final report in February 1971. The EC's commitment to a process that would eventually lead to full monetary union began to be widely recognized, not just within the Community. A speech on 'The City and Europe' in December 1971 by the Governor of the Bank of England, Leslie O'Brien, shortly after the votes in the UK Parliament to join the EEC, concluded with the following far-sighted prophecy:

> We are embarked on a journey which will ultimately lead to the emergence of a single currency system for the members of the European Community. We do not know quite how long that journey will take, and it is essentially the harmonisation of the domestic characteristics that will determine the answer. (Bank of England 1972, p. 86)

The Werner Report envisaged the creation of an economic and monetary union which would 'make it possible to realize an area in which goods and services, people and capital will circulate freely and without competitive distortions, without thereby giving rise to structural or regional disequilibrium' (Werner Report 1970, p. 9). The grand aim was to turn the common market into a single economy. However, little attempt was made by Werner or other official sources to rationalize EMU's contribution to this objective; it was largely taken for granted that a single economy called for, in effect, a single money.[4] The key requirements for EMU were held to be the irrevocable fixing of exchange rates (but there was no mention of a single currency); a central monetary authority and monetary policy; unified capital markets; determination of fiscal policy at Community level, including methods of financing, taxation, etc.; strengthening and centralization of the Community's regional and structural policies; and closer consultation among the social partners at the Community level.

This was an ambitious programme with more emphasis on fiscal centralization and cooperation with the social partners than would be fashionable nowadays. The achievement of EMU was envisaged in stages. The first stage, to be completed by end-1973, would focus on narrowing of exchange-rate margins, closer cooperation on domestic policies, and progress towards tax harmonization, particularly VAT. The second stage, the transition, was less defined, and no clear timetable was set, although the Report suggested that full EMU should be feasible by around 1980, given the political will. This programme was endorsed by the Paris Summit of October 1972, which called for its completion no later than end-1980.

Failure to achieve EMU on the Werner timetable has generally been attributed to external events which blew the process off course in the early 1970s, principally the switch from pegged exchange rates to floating in the global monetary system, and the first oil-price shock and the change in the economic environment it caused (Gros and Thygesen 1992). But recent reappraisals have emphasized internal weaknesses in the plan, especially 'insufficient constraints on national policies, institutional ambiguities, inappropriate policy conception and lack of internal momentum' (Baer and Padoa-Schioppa 1989, p. 56, in a paper for the Delors Committee). No doubt clearer definition of the new institutions and progression between stages would have helped, and the external shocks were important setbacks. But the Commission's leaders at the time also appear to have underestimated the reluctance of national political authorities to accept EC constraints on their policies, particularly in the tax, expenditure and regional fields, and especially when the economic environment deteriorated in the mid-1970s. A less ambitious programme concentrating on monetary and financial policies might have fared better – a lesson which the Delors Committee was to take to heart, albeit in more propitious circumstances.

Not all the Werner proposals fell by the wayside. By 1974 procedural changes had been made, such as more frequent (monthly) meetings of ECOFIN and discussion of monetary policy by the Monetary Committee and the Governors' Committee in Basle. However, the main innovation was in exchange-rate cooperation, through the introduction in 1972 by agreement at Basle of the so-called European currency 'snake', followed in 1973 by the establishment of the European Monetary Cooperation Fund. Then in 1974 came the *Council Decision on the attainment of a high degree of convergence of economic policies,* and the *Directive on stability, growth and full employment,* which nevertheless fell far short of the Werner recommendations for the first stage (Baer and Padoa-Schioppa 1989, p. 56).

The currency 'snake' was an arrangement to limit fluctuations between participants' exchange rates to ± 2.25%, half the corresponding margin for non-dollar currencies established under the Smithsonian Agreement in December 1971. It commenced with the EEC-6 currencies and was quickly joined by sterling, the Irish pound and the Danish and Norwegian kroner. However it soon ran into serious difficulties: sterling was forced out after only a brief period, and later the lira and French franc (twice, rejoining once). By 1978 it retained only five adherents, with the D-mark as the major currency and a few others, including (not as formal members) the Swiss franc and the Austrian schilling. It proved unsustainable because most participants were unwilling to take the tough policy measures needed to stabilize exchange rates in the face of the extreme currency pressures following the first oil shock. Nevertheless it was the first European attempt at a formal scheme to stabilize exchange rates and it left important pointers for the next effort at the end of the decade.

The European Monetary System

The process of European monetary integration resurfaced in the late 1970s, through an initiative by Chancellor Schmidt and President Giscard d'Estaing to create what became the European Monetary System (EMS), responding to Commission President Roy Jenkins's publicly expressed concerns about the Community losing its way and his call for revival of EMU as a grand objective (Jenkins 1977). The basic motivation was, however, the demise of Bretton Woods, the failure of the dollar as an international standard, and the emergence in Germany of 'a new national monetary self-interest in the goal of external stability' (Dyson 1994, p. 98). The declared objective (in a Franco-German paper for the Bremen European Council of July 1978) was relatively modest: to create 'a zone of monetary stability in Europe' by stabilizing exchange rates; there was no mention of monetary union. Thygesen (1993, p. 5) notes that 'when the EMS was negotiated in 1978 any reference to advanced forms of monetary integration was carefully avoided'. At this time, he says, 'the idea of a common monetary policy under free capital flows and, ultimately, a single currency, was too remote from current realities to return to the agenda'. Nevertheless the goal of EMU had not been abandoned and, prompted by papers from the Commission, the European

Councils of November 1976 and December 1977 made low-key affirmations of EMU as the ultimate goal. With only two years to go before the original target for completing the second 'Werner' stage, the European Council of December 1978 called for the establishment of a European Monetary Fund (intended to support the EMS) and for the use of the ECU as a reserve asset. This led to several reports by 'wise men' and draft action plans in the early 1980s. The outcome was the chapter on EMU in the Single European Act of 1985, which committed EC governments to creating monetary union as a necessary step towards full exploitation of the Single Market.

The EMS came into operation in March 1979. Much has been written about the operation and effects of its central apparatus, the Exchange Rate Mechanism (ERM).[5] Research suggests that the ERM brought about a major increase in exchange stability among participants after a few years, although at some cost to stability against currencies outside the system. It is less clear that the ERM promoted greater stability of *real* exchange rates (nominal rates adjusted for relative inflation), and some critics maintain that adherence to the mechanism ultimately led to unsustainable real rates, especially after 1987 when governments unwisely suppressed realignments (Williamson 1993a, p. 195).

Three phases have been identified in the EMS's development. First, there was a phase of about four years to 1983, during which reliance on exchange-rate changes was reduced but not eliminated. There were frequent realignments, in which the weaker currencies moved most (e.g. against the dollar), but devaluations tended not to compensate fully for inflation and the concept of 'asymmetric' policy gained ground – i.e. that the onus for corrective action (monetary tightening) lay with weak-currency members. The perception arose that ERM membership could be a means not merely of stabilizing exchange rates, but also of securing price stability.

There then occurred a second phase of about six years in which realignments became less frequent as policies in the weak-currency economies became more oriented towards stability against the D-mark, increasingly accepted as the system's 'anchor' currency by virtue of persistently low inflation in West Germany. The belief grew that governments with weak inflationary reputations could gain credibility rapidly and painlessly by committing themselves to a fixed exchange rate against the low-inflation currencies, provided they were prepared to emulate their monetary policy, which essentially meant adopting German short-term interest rates, plus a premium for uncertainty demanded by the markets. This phase saw a large and sustained fall in inflation among ERM participants (as may be seen from Table 7.1) – although some non-ERM members performed just as well. Economists differ on how far disinflation in the ERM economies was due to an inherent improvement in agents' behaviour (lower inflation expectations, more labour-market flexibility) and how far simply to the more determined pursuit of anti-inflation policies, backed by the clear political commitment to a firm exchange rate.

This phase developed into an even more ambitious one towards the end of the 1980s in which the ERM came to be seen as the prelude – some called it the 'ante-room' or 'glide path' – to EMU, and markets became convinced that maintaining the ERM parity was a policy priority for all participants, including the United Kingdom after it joined in October 1990. Belief grew in a 'hard' ERM with progressively narrower margins and no further realignments. So long as those commitments remained credible, the markets were prepared to overlook doubts about the long-term sustainability of existing parities despite persistent, albeit narrowing, gaps between national inflation rates (Giavazzi and Spaventa, 1990). The emerging success of the negotiations in the EMU IGC, and the expectation that a currency's stability within the ERM would be a test of eligibility for EMU, boosted market confidence. So too did the Basle–Nyborg agreement of 1987, which strengthened the system by providing for (voluntary) intramarginal intervention and extending the 'very short-term financing facility' (VSTF).

However, this mood in the markets did not last. From early 1992, several developments combined to challenge the credibility of ERM commitments in a number of States: a sharp tightening of monetary policy in the 'anchor' country, in response to the problems created by German reunification; a simultaneous weakening of the US dollar reflecting policy relaxation there, which intensified competitive pressure on exposed currencies, notably sterling; and referenda results which cast doubt on the momentum towards EMU, even in France. The consequences in the form of the ERM crises of autumn 1992 and summer 1993 are well known. As market doubts grew about willingness in the weaker-currency States to accept the monetary stringency implied by Bundesbank policies, intense downward pressure developed against their currencies – the Nordics on the fringes of the EMS and the weaker ones within it (the peseta, the escudo, the Irish pound) – all of which had to devalue at least once; the lira and sterling, which were forced out of the ERM in September 1992; and later the Danish krone and eventually even the French and Belgian francs, which came under intense pressure in the summer of 1993 despite continued market faith in their sound 'fundamentals'. These pressures subsided only after the massive widening of the ERM fluctuation bands to ±15% in August 1993, which effectively removed the self-fulfilling one-way bets that had hitherto fuelled speculation. There was then a period of relative stability until early 1995, when equally severe currency turbulence revisited EC currencies within and outside the ERM, as will be seen in Chapter 7.

These upsets have led to considerable heart-searching among EC policymakers about the role and operation of the ERM. The UK government's view that it is fatally flawed was not well received initially, but in due course official recommendations for modest reforms were put forward by the EC Monetary Committee and the Governors' Committee. These focused on improved monitoring of exchange-rate and associated developments, better policy consultation, more timely action to adjust policies when existing ones are judged inappropriate, and greater willingness to realign when existing central rates are judged not sustainable. It was conceded too that there were faults in the VSTF, although prospective remedies remain unclear. For the time being there remains little disposition to restore narrower bands formally or carry out reforms, and the role of the mechanism in the approach to EMU is highly uncertain.

The Delors Report

When confidence was high before the ERM crises, the view that the final route to EMU led via a hard ERM was boosted by the publication of the Delors Report in 1989.[6] The drive towards a harder ERM had gained momentum with the agreement in 1986 to move rapidly to the Single Market, and there was a surge of support for EMU, with the ERM as entry route, at the top of the French and German governments (Thygesen 1993, p. 5). ECOFIN's decision in June 1988 on a timetable to remove all remaining exchange controls among Member States opened the way for the Hanover European Council later that month to appoint a Committee chaired by Jacques Delors, President of the Commission, and comprising mainly the EC central-bank governors, to produce a blueprint for EMU on the working assumption of a favourable political decision. The Committee reported in April 1989 and its recommendations were endorsed by the Madrid European Council in June, which took the political decisions to start Stage I of the Delors process on 1 July 1990 and convene an IGC on EMU as soon as possible thereafter.

Despite a fairly critical reception in the financial press, the Delors Report was to be a dominant influence on the negotiations in the EMU IGC. Its three-stage approach was on Werner lines, but more specific about the institutions needed, and about progression between stages.[7] The European System of Central Banks it proposed for Stage III was close to that adopted in the Treaty and Statute (Committee for the Study of Economic and Monetary Union 1989, pp. 25–7). It went further than Werner in calling for a *single currency* and for *binding rules* on fiscal policy and financing in Stage III, including 'effective upper limits on budget deficits' and no monetary financing (p. 28). While stressing the importance of free capital movements, stronger competition policy, an extension of Community policies to reduce regional disparities, and better coordination of macroeconomic policy, it stopped short of the centralization recommended by Werner. However, for Stage II it was relatively ambitious, recommending a medium-term framework for policy which would facilitate 'intervening when significant deviations occurred' (p. 38) and establishment of the ESCB with policy functions which 'would gradually evolve as experience was gained'. In the event its plans for an embryo central bank in Stage II with a policy-coordinating role were not accepted, as will be seen.

Although the Delors Committee was more specific than Werner in many ways, it did not develop an economic rationale of EMU, as Thygesen (1989) admits. This was understandable, given its terms of reference, which requested a technical blueprint, not an economic study. Less defensible was the Report's reluctance to consider alternative routes to EMU, apart from a brief review of the parallel currency approach, which despite a respectable European pedigree received rather summary dismissal (p. 33).

Conclusions

The Community's interest in EMU is long-standing. The sustained pursuit of a highly ambitious economic objective is a notable manifestation of commitment by successive European leaders. Some commentators have suggested that it is proof that the Community is ready to move to full EMU without further delay: 'Our own view, supported by the historical analysis, is that all the building blocks for MU have been identified and are lined up on the construction site, ready for assembly' (Papadia and Saccomanni 1994, p. 68). This seems a debatable view; and the claim by these authors (p. 58) that the EMU process represents the revealed preferences of European citizens appears somewhat fanciful. EMU involves complex economic issues, and it is questionable how accurately the effects can be gauged by experts, let alone ordinary citizens. More plausible is the view, generally endorsed by economists among others, that the EMU campaign over the years has been driven mainly by *political* objectives: closer political union, for which a single currency would be a vital prop; the French ambition to lock reunified Germany more securely into the Community via stronger economic ties; and the general wish outside Germany to 'collectivize' the formulation of monetary policy, which under a hard ERM is dictated by the interests of the 'anchor' economy (Tyrie 1991).

In contrast, the economic rationale behind EMU has been vague, although it gathered force when the traditional Francocentric quest for a zone of monetary stability in Europe was joined in the 1970s by German concerns to minimize the D-mark's exposure to dollar instability after the demise of Bretton Woods, as Dyson and others have recalled. The fact that EMU has remained elusive for so long reflects not only institutional problems – the 'hollow core' that political scientists detect at the heart of the EMU process, due to its dependence on the reluctant leadership of the Bundesbank (Dyson 1994, Chapter 9) – but also diversity of EC States' economic objectives and performance, which only now seems to be narrowing, and perhaps only among the core States. The non-realization of the Werner plan and the undoing of attempts to fix exchange rates in the 'snake' and the narrow-band ERM, and renewed currency turbulence more recently, raise legitimate questions about the sustainability of an edifice designed to lock European exchange rates permanently together. Nevertheless history also shows that EMU is not a passing fashion; the precedents are too insistent to permit that view. Contrary to some perceptions, the Community is unlikely to be sidetracked by currency turbulence or inadequate convergence among its weaker economies, or even to attenuate the Maastricht timetable much, now that the countdown to EMU has begun.

Chapter 4

Is the EC an optimal currency area?

The principles relating to the size and characteristics of currency areas have long interested economists. The essential problem has been to find a rationale for the existence of separate currencies, given that trade generally enhances prosperity and that a single money facilitates trade. Not surprisingly, the explanation turns on the fact that neighbouring regions may have very different economic characteristics, so that (for example) shocks affect them differently. If wages and prices are not fully flexible and resources not fully mobile, adjustment may be assisted by changes in interregional exchange rates. Such changes of course require separate currencies.

The traditional theory

The theoretical debate began in the early 1960s when it was asked whether some types of country would benefit from leaving the Bretton Woods regime. Later, the main stimulus became Europe's developing interest in monetary integration. The question then was whether it would be advantageous for groups of countries to lock their exchange rates permanently, and if so what the membership of the 'optimal currency area' would be. At that stage, the benefits from belonging to a currency area were largely taken for granted; the analysis concentrated on the possible costs.

In the classic article that began the debate, Mundell (1961) showed that unless labour and capital can move freely between regions, a shock which shifts global demand from the products of one region to those of another will create unemployment in the former if (nominal) wages and prices there are rigid and its exchange rate is fixed. In these circumstances devaluation may mitigate the fall in employment in the disadvantaged region. Then McKinnon (1963) showed that the effectiveness of the exchange rate for restoring external balance in an economy adversely affected by an external-demand shock is likely to be greater the less open it is to foreign trade: in an economy with a small tradable sector, the exchange-rate change needed to transfer a given quantity of resources into tradables will be relatively small, and the effects on domestic inflation minor. Later Kenen (1969) showed that the impact of a given shock to demand or to supply (affecting relative costs) on an economy's total output will be smaller, the greater the variety of products it produces. Economies that specialize in a limited range of products thus have a greater need for exchange-rate flexibility, although the extent to which this will enable them to preserve employment in the face of a shock will depend on how readily labour and capital can move internally between industries.

In summary, the traditional literature suggested four criteria for judging whether regions should form a currency area: mobility of factors of production, flexibility of prices and wages, openness to trade and diversity of production. Regions that have relatively closed economies, narrow product ranges, strong price and wage rigidities, and low external mobility of labour and capital should not join monetary unions, but should instead retain exchange-rate flexibility, assuming they have some *internal* factor mobility.

However, it is far from easy to translate these broad principles into operational criteria or prescribe their relative importance. In subsequent assessments the traditional literature has usually been judged inconclusive for practical purposes, if anything supporting a presumption against the creation of large currency unions. Kenen (1969) nevertheless concluded that mature industrial economies might successfully lock their exchange rates under certain conditions: 'Fixed rates, I believe, are most appropriate – or least inappropriate — to well-diversified national economies,' (p. 54). He stressed that they would need 'potent and sophisticated internal policies', particularly 'close control over money wage rates, or at least be able to align the rate of change with rates of change prevailing abroad' and 'a wide array of budgetary policies to deal with stubborn "pockets of unemployment"' (ibid.).

Subsequent commentators have pointed out that Kenen's criterion of product diversity suggests that large economies like France and Germany should form a currency area, since they are likely to be highly diversified (Corden 1993, p. 9). However, this criterion in isolation might appear to imply the improbable conclusion that the whole world should form a currency area, since it would be maximally diversified (ibid., p. 10). Corden's answer to that conundrum was to put forward a distinction between *optimal* and *'feasible'* currency areas, where feasibility depends on the effectiveness of the exchange rate as an adjustment device. Large currency areas may be feasible, but not necessarily optimal. The key problem for very large currency areas is likely to be insufficient mobility of production factors, especially labour, as Kenen continues to stress.[1] (An associated problem is that a single currency may promote greater regional specialization, as Krugman has pointed out in commenting on US experience – as will be explained later.) These complications illustrate the inadequacy of the theoretical criteria in isolation and the need to supplement them with empirical assessments.

Recent theorists have reached similarly agnostic conclusions. Krugman (1990) follows McKinnon in stressing openness to trade as a key criterion. Switching from floating to fixed exchange rates confers benefits in the form of 'decreased uncertainty and confusion about the values of national moneys' and incurs costs in the form of 'increased difficulty of adjusting relative prices'; once openness exceeds a certain level, fixed exchange rates become preferable to floating. But Krugman warns that the approach is somewhat speculative, because 'both the cost and the benefit depend on the unit of account function of money', which he describes as a 'bounded rationality issue' (i.e. an issue where rational behaviour is subject to important information constraints). On EMU he sees a lack of hard evidence that optimal currency areas are intermediate in size between a large country and the world:

> We actually have no particular reason to suppose that Europe is the
> right size for a monetary union. At one extreme one could claim
> that the whole world constitutes the optimal currency area. This is a
> fairly popular position at the moment, under the influence of global
> monetarists like McKinnon, and it is also a safe position, since it is
> not going to happen.... The contrary position is near-heresy in the
> current political climate, but it is perfectly possible to make a case
> that Europe is too large for monetary union to be desirable.
> (Krugman 1990, pp. 192–3)

He offers several arguments for that case. First, the EC is not exceptionally integrated via trade; the intra-Community trade of the four major economies averages only 15% of GNP, less than Canada's trade with the

USA, yet Canada has not made monetary union a priority. Secondly, exchange-rate changes can clearly affect relative wage rates within Europe – 'one need only look at the United Kingdom's roller-coaster competitiveness from the mid-1970s to the mid-1980s as a demonstration'. Thirdly, labour mobility among EC economies is hardly enough to provide much of an alternative to exchange-rate adjustment. He also notes that the United States itself may not be an optimal currency area, and concludes that although the traditional literature provides insights, it is 'very far from giving an operational guide to policy' (ibid., p. 193).

These arguments lead Krugman and others to the view that the driving motives behind EMU are essentially political; a single currency both creates and symbolizes community of interest, hence the priority given to EMU by those who seek political union in Europe. This emphasis on EMU as a politically motivated exercise is not uncommon among economists, even those who also believe that the economic motives themselves are substantial.

Policy coordination and credibility

Since the early 1970s theoretical attention has shifted more to monetary policy. McKinnon had already argued that optimality should include internal price stability as an objective, along with stability of income/employment and external balance, and one of his conclusions was that an open economy might best achieve price stability by linking its currency to a strong external currency (McKinnon 1963, p. 722). Others challenged this view, pointing out that countries might give different weights to policy objectives such as high employment and price stability and this might lead them to adopt different positions on their Phillips curves (the curve representing the trade-off between unemployment and wages). They might also face different trade-offs, owing to institutional or behavioural differences in their economies. If so, fixing their exchange rates might imply significant costs to 'internal balance' (Corden 1972).

A standard assumption at the time was that there is a tradeoff between unemployment and inflation in the long run as well as the short run, but few mainstream economists would now accept this. More recently Corden has argued (1993) that similar conclusions still apply on the assumption that a trade-off exists only in the short run, which is what most economists now accept – characterized in the literature as the 'inflation-augmented Phillips curve'. But the costs of currency union under this assumption will be less, because a monetary policy which seeks to move an economy up its short-term Phillips curve has adverse long-term effects on inflation expectations which make the policy less appealing.

The widespread introduction of rational expectations as a behavioural assumption into economic theory in the past two decades has transformed the policy arguments on monetary integration, as in many other fields, by bringing policy *credibility* to the fore.[2] The essential idea is that wage and price setters learn through experience to anticipate fully the effects of governments' 'anti-equilibrium' policies, with the result that price expectations change abruptly as soon as any incentive develops for governments to adopt such policies. Then, very quickly, the Phillips curve shifts so that actual unemployment does not deviate, or does so only very temporarily, from the 'natural rate' (the rate at which there is no tendency for inflation to change). In the extreme case, where expectations are based on perfect foresight and wages and prices adjust instantaneously to the new equilibrium level, there is not even a short-term trade-off and the government ceases to be able to influence the level of employment. However, markets may not be convinced that the government will resist all temptations to expand activity, even when there is no trade-off, and the economy will then have to pay a penalty in terms of persistently higher inflation than under a government with a high anti-inflation reputation. Governments with suspect policy reputations are accordingly under pressure either to demonstrate policy consistency over a long period, or to short-circuit that process by adopting rules that tie their own hands. The question in the present context is whether joining a monetary union will help policy credibility (De Grauwe 1992). The corresponding question also arose in relation to ERM membership.

Theory on its own cannot resolve this question. The answer must depend, in the case of the ERM, on the existence of an 'anchor currency' run by monetary authorities of impeccable reputation and political independence. In the past, Germany with the Bundesbank has played that role, but as Krugman (1990) observed, it cannot be relied on to do so indefinitely. On the face of it, EMU offers a better prospect because it involves a stronger commitment, with realignment ruled out by treaty, and institutional arrangements hard to unscramble, once firmly established – provided the central monetary institution has a strong price stability mandate set within an unassailable constitution.

Even so the superiority of EMU over the ERM in this respect cannot be guaranteed. Whereas the ERM developed as a tacit arrangement in which the thrust of monetary policy was determined by the authorities in the least inflation-prone country, EMU's much more explicit arrangements are likely to mean that all participants acquire some influence on policy. Thus EMU could turn out to be more symmetrical than the ERM, and its credibility less than that of at least the core of the ERM.

Furthermore the rational-expectations model, although common in the literature, is an extreme case. In the real world there are likely to be sufficient imperfections of knowledge and wage/price rigidities to mean that monetary (and fiscal) policy can affect activity in the short and even medium terms, as experience shows. In that case governments with plural economic objectives may prefer to retain more policy sovereignty than is available under a tightly constituted EMU designed to give overwhelming priority to price stability. On the other hand, if the constitution of EMU leaves enough flexibility to pursue a measure of short-term stabilization within a strong medium-term commitment to price stability, many governments might find it an attractive compromise.

Not all economists would be content with so open a conclusion. Those who believe that labour markets in modern economies display a high degree of rational expectations, and that national policy-makers in most have a serious problem to convince markets of their ability to run time-consistent, non-accommodating monetary policies, see a strong case for EMU among countries as industrially and financially integrated as the EC. For example, Bofinger (1994): 'The credibility of monetary policy can be strengthened by extending the size of currency areas beyond the size of national states. The transfer of monetary policy responsibilities to the supranational level reduces the influence of national policy makers' (p. 39).

Protagonists of the modern 'sound money' school believe that the optimal-currency literature as reinterpreted by Krugman and others gives insufficient weight to the monetary-policy advantages of EMU. They claim benefits beyond superior policy coordination and credibility: as economies become more open, workers lose money illusion and become more conscious of the real income effects of currency depreciation, so it is no longer appropriate to assume downward rigidity of nominal wages (Bofinger 1994, pp. 44-7). Furthermore, asymmetric shocks that result from divergent national monetary policies would be eliminated under EMU. These monetary arguments go to the heart of the Commission's case for EMU, considered in the next chapter.

Network externalities and switching costs

Both the traditional theory of currency unions and its monetary extensions have tended to take for granted the microeconomic benefits of a single money for trade and exchange, but modern theorists are revisiting these issues, drawing on earlier work relating to the benefits of standardization from using a single money. For example, it is suggested that money confers 'network externalities' on its users, defined as 'network effects whereby the value of a particular currency depends on how many others use it as well' (Dowd and Greenaway 1993, p. 1180). This concept appears to be a generalized version of the transactions and information benefits identified in empirical work on EMU, discussed in the next chapter. Other things being equal – which may be an important qualification when regional characteristics differ, as the traditional theory showed – per capita welfare derived from a currency's use will increase with the number of agents using it. The existence of separate currencies despite this feature is attributed to several factors: historical circumstances; uncertainties about the potential benefits from changing to a new currency, including the number of agents ultimately likely to use it; and the 'switching costs' of converting to a new currency, including learning and adaptation costs to private individuals as well as system costs to firms and governments.

These uncertainties and costs tend to create inertia in the use of separate currencies which may be quite hard to overcome, even if it is recognized that considerable social benefits could arise from switching to a new currency. They help to explain the continued survival of 'inferior' currencies in many high-inflation economies, despite the difficulties they create for financing ordinary transactions. They also suggest why 'parallel' currencies are rare; their *non-network* advantages have to be major and widely recognized before individuals voluntarily adopt them. It follows, according to these theories, that there may be a role for public authorities to take administrative action to introduce a new currency, overcoming inertia if the step would contribute to long-run efficiency. Moreover, they suggest that if there are important switching costs which depend on the number of citizens using the currency, it may be preferable to switch to a successful existing currency if one is available, rather than to introduce a totally new one. There are clearly significant messages for EMU from these new lines of thought.

Evidence on currency areas

Openness to trade
Of the four main criteria developed in the traditional literature, the least difficult to measure is trade openness. As with all the criteria, however, there remains the question of the appropriate standard of comparison.

Table 4.1: Openness to trade, EC-12 States, USA and Japan, 1991–4 (%)[a]

Country	Intra-EC[b]	Total[c]	EC share[d]
Belgium/Luxembourg	40.4	68.9	73.7
Ireland	36.4	59.1	70.8
Netherlands	28.8	50.2	67.1
Portugal	21.7	34.2	74.1
Greece	13.8	28.2	63.3
Denmark	13.1	32.9	51.8
Germany[e]	11.6	29.1	51.8
UK	10.5	24.9	52.2
France	10.3	21.7	59.9
Spain	9.7	20.0	64.7
Italy	8.9	20.5	57.4
EC-12	12.9	27.5	59.7
USA		11.0	
Japan		8.7	

[a] Annual averages, 1991–4. 1993 partly estimated; 1994 Commission forecasts.
[b] Share of intra-EC trade, (Exports + Imports)/2 in GDP at current market prices, goods only. Foreign Trade Statistics.
[c] Share of total trade, (Exports + Imports)/2 in GDP at current market prices, goods and services. National-accounts definitions.
[d] Share of intra-EC in total trade, goods only.
[e] Former West Germany.
Source: Calculated from Commission of the European Communities (1993b), Statistical Annex.

Most analyses approach that problem by taking large existing currency unions as benchmarks – usually the USA, although there are questions about the validity of that standard, as Krugman noted.

Trade data for the EC-12 economies in 1991–4 are summarized in Table 4.1, which ranks countries in descending order of openness to *intra*-EC trade (goods only, see column [1]). On this measure openness differs widely, from around 40% (average of imports and exports to GDP) in two small economies down to around 10% in the five large ones. There is clearly a strong positive correlation between this intra-EC measure and the wider measure shown in column (2), which refers to total trade (including services, and trade with non-EC countries). Since the question at stake here is EMU in the Community, the intra-EC measure is more relevant. Column (3) shows intra-EC trade as a share of total trade (goods only). There is a tendency for smaller countries to do more of their trade with the rest of the EC: the (unweighted) average of this measure for Benelux, Ireland, Portugal and Greece is nearly 70%, compared with a (weighted) average for EC-12 of just under 60%.

It would be instructive to compare the openness of the 12 EC States with the corresponding openness of major regions of the United States (i.e. intra-USA), but unfortunately trade data for US regions are not readily available. The aggregate US measure shown in column (2), 11%, is relevant, however. It appears that, although on average EC States do modestly more intra-EC trade (after allowing for services) than the USA does with the rest of the world, the five largest countries individually do not do much more. On this criterion, if the USA is an optimal currency area *vis-à-vis* the rest of the world (i.e. should float against it), the large countries of the EC could be similarly positioned *vis-à-vis* the rest of the EC (i.e. they also should individually float). On the other hand, most of the small EC countries are much more open to EC trade than the USA is to global trade and on that criterion look too small to be optimal currency areas. There is a suggestion here of tension between the interests of the large and small EC States, the latter being more suited to fixed-rate arrangements. Moreover the openness of the EC-12 *to the rest of the world*, 8.7% on a goods-only basis (derived from columns [1] and [3]) is the same as that of Japan, and not very different from that of the USA. Thus if the USA and Japan are each optimal currency areas, the EC *collectively* may also be one – even if some countries are more suited to joining than others.

Although the United Kingdom, like other EC economies, is clearly a more open economy in terms of total trade than the USA (or Japan), it is not noticeably more open to EC trade (at 10.5%, or around 12.5% including services) than the USA is to global trade. Thus on openness grounds the UK may be an optimal currency area *vis-à-vis* the EC, so it is not obvious on this criterion that the UK should join EMU. Moreover since much of Ireland's trade is with the UK, it would do better on this criterion to re-form monetary union with the latter if it does not join EMU. Other criteria might of course point to other conclusions.

Diversity of production

Data on output composition between major industrial sectors are available for manufacturing in individual EC States and for the 12 Federal Reserve Districts of the USA, although not in comparable detail for wider production aggregates. They have been analysed in a widely noted

Figure 4.1: Regional unemployment disparities: US states and DC (1992) and EU Level 1 regions (1993)

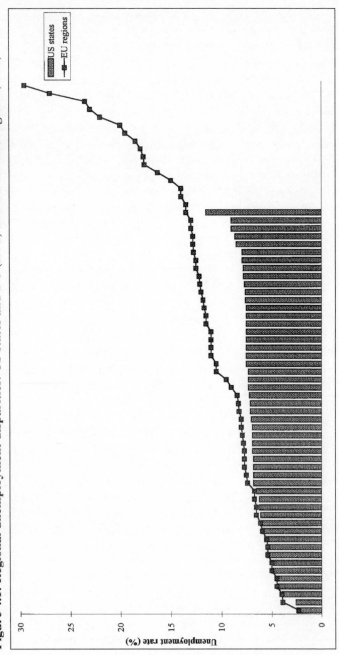

Source: US Department of Commerce; Eurostat. Updated from Begg and Mayes (1993).

study by Bini-Smaghi and Vori (1992) which investigated several key characteristics of the EC as an optimal currency area. They conclude for the 1980s that, 'on average, the differences between regional production structures are much larger within the US than within the EC. EC national economies are much more alike than US regions' (p. 86). Interregional dispersion of industry shares in total output in the USA is about twice the average in the EC-12. It also appears that dispersion among the EC-6 (the founder members) is markedly lower than among the EC-12. On this evidence, EC economies are less likely to suffer from differential shocks (disturbances that have different effects on economies with different characteristics) than US regions.

A similar conclusion was found by Krugman (1992), using more broadly aggregated regions; his explanation was that lower transport costs, transactions costs and regulatory differences in the common market of the USA have led to progressively greater geographic concentration of industry there. Thus on Kenen's criterion, the present-day EC is likely to be more suited to form a currency area than the USA: on this measure, it should be less prone than the USA to asymmetric shocks, and interregional exchange rates should be a less effective means of adjustment in the EC they would be in the USA.

Mobility of labour
Labour mobility cannot be measured directly. Studies tend to focus on interregional differences in unemployment rates, on the assumption that migration is driven by the search for employment. The consensus is that labour is much more mobile within the USA than within the EC (OECD 1986; Eichengreen 1990b). Eichengreen cites a study which concluded that mobility in the USA was some two to three times that within individual European countries, measured by the proportion of population changing region of residence; and mobility between European countries is even lower. This finding is consistent with the evidence from unemployment, which shows that the dispersion between national unemployment rates in the Community is much larger than between major US regions (see Figure 4.1).

Bini-Smaghi and Vori (1992, Table 6) report similar results for 1990. However, they also note that the dispersion of unemployment rates *within* EC States has latterly become relatively high: in 1990, it was higher within Italy, Spain and the UK than *between* EC states; and while it was still lower within Germany, France and the Netherlands than between the EC-12, it was at least as high as between the EC-6. They

31

reason from this that the larger EC countries may not benefit much from flexible exchange rates, recalling the traditional analysis (because their domestic economies may not adjust readily to exchange-rate signals). If so, the general conclusion they and others have drawn from the labour-market evidence needs to be qualified somewhat; the evidence nevertheless suggests that the EC is less likely than the USA to be an optimal currency area on this criterion.

Wage and price flexibility

Efforts have been made to examine the difficult subject of *wage and price flexibility*, distinguishing between nominal and real flexibility. Bruno and Sachs (1985) concluded that real wages are more rigid in Europe than in the USA, whereas the reverse is true of nominal wages. If so, nominal exchange-rate adjustment should be more effective in the USA than Europe, which should place greater reliance on other devices to cope with asymmetric shocks, and take steps to improve labour-market flexibility. Bini-Smaghi and Vori (1992) also support this conclusion. They report (Table 6) a set of OECD estimates of the elasticity of nominal wages with respect to prices and to unemployment rates in major industrial countries; in eight EC economies for which estimates were available, the wage/price elasticity is higher than in the USA or Canada – and in two (Germany, Italy) much higher; whereas European wage/unemployment elasticities are much smaller than US and Canadian elasticities. Their derived index of real-wage rigidity is greater than unity in all eight EC countries, and very high in Germany, whereas in the USA and Canada it is only one-fifth and one-third respectively. They conclude that unless real-wage rigidity falls in the EC, regional exchange rates will be less effective in ameliorating shocks there than they would be within the USA and Canada.

Asymmetric shocks

There have also been exercises to examine the nature of shocks affecting the European and North American economies. Issues investigated include whether they are symmetric (i.e. affect different economies uniformly) or asymmetric (affect economies differently); whether they are temporary or permanent; whether they are nominal or real; and whether they originate internally or externally. The results are not easy to summarize. Cohen and Wyplosz (1989) examined shocks in France and Germany and concluded that symmetric shocks dominate the asymmetric ones, and tend to be permanent rather than temporary. They also found that when

France and Germany in combination are compared with the United States, asymmetric shocks tend to dominate the symmetric ones. (The impact of a shock may depend on whether the industrial structures in the affected countries are similar, as .well as on the shock itself.) They conclude that a monetary union would be more appropriate between France and Germany than between 'Europe' and the USA.[3]

Bini-Smaghi and Vori (1992) report an exercise which correlates GDP movements in EC Member States with those in the rest of the EC through the period 1963–89, whether measured as deviations from a linear trend or as first differences; a corresponding exercise was undertaken for the 12 US Federal Reserve Districts. They find (Table 2) that the GDPs of the EC-6 move more uniformly than those of the US Districts, regardless of whether the whole period or the period 1979–89 is considered. (Weber [1991] also finds that shocks to inflation and other nominal variables have uniform effects between EMS countries.) But the EC movements become less uniform when new members, especially the United Kingdom and Denmark, are included, and in the period 1979–89 the US movements are more uniform. This suggests that the impacts of shocks among the newer Member States are distinctly less uniform than among the old.

A study by Bayoumi and Eichengreen (1992) using a different methodology reaches rather stronger but not dissimilar conclusions. Unlike the studies cited above, the methodology of structural auto-regression enables them to distinguish underlying shocks from the responses to them, whether behavioural or policy-induced, which simple correlation analysis cannot do. They classify shocks according to whether they originate on the demand or supply side; supply shocks are defined as having permanent effects on output and the price level, whereas demand shocks have permanent effects only on the price level. Annual data 1962–88 were used for 11 EC States and 8 standard regions of the USA.

Their main result is that whereas supply shocks affecting the EC are highly correlated between Germany and four of its close neighbours, the correlation is much lower between Germany and 'the periphery' (Italy, Spain, Ireland, the United Kingdom, Portugal and Greece). There is a somewhat similar pattern in the USA – a clear distinction between the mid-east and four neighbouring regions, between which supply shocks are fairly highly correlated, and more distant US regions, where shocks are more independent. An analogous distinction between core and periphery, if not quite so pronounced, exists for demand shocks, both in the EC and the USA. The results are illustrated in Figure 4.2, where for

33

Figure 4.2: Correlation of demand and supply shocks with anchor areas[a]

(a) EC countries[b]

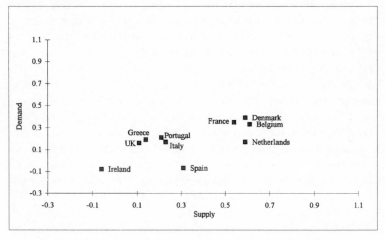

(b) US regions[c]

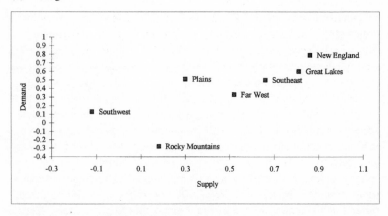

Source: Bayoumi and Eichengreen 1992, Chart 4.

[a] Shocks are measured as the residuals in vector auto-regression equations, in which current rates of change of output and prices are regressed on their lagged values. See Bayoumi and Eichengreen (1992), pp. 12–17.
[b] Correlation of national supply and demand disturbances with German supply and demand disturbances.
[c] Correlation of regional supply and demand disturbances with supply and demand disturbances of Mid-east region.

example the closeness of the scatter between the core EC States indicates the high degree of correlation with Germany in their experience of both types of shock.

A corresponding dichotomy also emerges within the EC when these authors examine the *size* of shocks, with peripheral countries experiencing much larger ones than core countries. Supply shocks among all the US regions are similar in magnitude to those experienced by the EC core, but demand shocks affecting US regions are somewhat larger than those affecting EC countries. Adjustment to shocks is faster in the USA than in Europe. They conclude that the 'European Community may find it more difficult to operate a monetary union than the United States'; in particular, the dichotomy in shock experience between the EC core and its periphery 'suggests that Germany and its immediate EC neighbours come much closer than the Community as a whole to representing a workable monetary union along American lines' (Bayoumi and Eichengreen 1992, p. 36).

Conclusions

The evidence on the EU's credentials as an optimal currency area is somewhat conflicting, according to the criterion looked at. Even if the comparisons with the USA were less varied, there is still the question whether the USA itself is an optimal currency area. The most that can be claimed with confidence is that it is a *feasible* currency area in Corden's sense, but that may depend on the operation of federal policies for which there is no close counterpart in the EU – a point taken up in later chapters.

There is the problem too, as several researchers have noted, that the empirical evidence inevitably reflects past experience, whereas the European economies are changing under the stimulus of the Single Market and the prospect of EMU. Conclusions based on past industrial structures or labour-market behaviour might cease to hold in time, when the new policy regimes take effect. These qualifications have to be born in mind in assessing the research but, unfortunately, they point in more than one direction: as Krugman observed, greater economic integration in the EC may lead in due course to greater specialization, and therefore greater proneness to asymmetric shocks. But as Bofinger argues, increased trade openness in the EC may decrease money illusion and improve labour-market flexibility; while capital-market integration there may increase the susceptibility of EC exchange rates to monetary shocks which have little to do with real-economy fundamentals.

The evidence on trade openness and on production diversity suggests that the Community as a whole could form a monetary union which is feasible in the sense that it could survive, but it might not be optimal. Collectively, the EC is about as open as the USA, and its Member States display more uniform industrial structures than do the regions of the USA, although this could change in time. On the face of it, the evidence on wage and price flexibility also seems to point against retaining flexible exchange rates, in that real wages seem more rigid in Europe than in America. However, this may be a treacherous conclusion: the USA may be able to survive as a currency area without extreme tensions only because it has other mechanisms of economic adjustment, for example federal fiscal policy; the EC may have greater need for exchange-rate flexibility because it lacks those central mechanisms. Despite the fact that real wages are comparatively rigid in most EU States, there is evidently enough flexibility in some to allow currency depreciations to deliver large and persistent changes in relative labour costs. This may not be an optimal mode of adjustment, because of the inflationary penalties, but it may be better than output deflation if that is the only alternative.

In contrast, the evidence on labour mobility tells mainly against the EU's suitability for EMU. Labour is much less mobile between EU States than between US or Canadian regions. Even this conclusion is not without its critics. Bini-Smaghi and Vori (1992) doubt that migration would be a socially acceptable adjustment mechanism in the EU, even if labour were more mobile. They argue that lack of labour mobility is not a relevant obstacle to EMU; the Community can find other ways of coping with shocks, such as regional policies to attract investment into disadvantaged areas. This seems a questionable argument. Mundell's original thesis still applies: if labour is immobile across national boundaries for whatever reasons, including potential social costs, countries should not abandon exchange-rate flexibility unless there are important countervailing benefits.

The evidence on shocks suggests that there may be little to choose between the EU as a whole and the USA as *feasible* currency areas: they seem to be subject to shocks of about the same magnitude on average. Whether they are optimal currency areas is more questionable. There is a fairly strong suggestion, certainly from Bayoumi and Eichengreen, that neither area is uniform across regions in response to shocks, and that the core group of six countries in the EU-12, focusing on Germany, is markedly different from the peripheral six. This result is supported in the work by Bini-Smaghi and Vori on disturbances to GDP, and it also finds echoes in their work on wage flexibility, which suggests that real-wage rigidity is greater in Germany than elsewhere, and that production diversity is larger among the EC core than among the peripheral States. Moreover the evidence on trade openness also supports a distinction between the small economies neighbouring Germany and the larger States, which are less open to EC trade. The United Kingdom is clearly in the 'peripheral but large' category; in particular, its experience of both demand and supply shocks has tended to be very different from that of the EC core.

Overall, the evidence gives some qualified support to the view that the EU-12 could form a monetary union which could survive, but it is not clear that such a union would be optimal. Whereas the core of the EU, comprising the smaller economies clustered around Germany, and possibly France, might well take smoothly to EMU, there are more or less serious questions about the candidacy of the rest, including Britain, Italy and Spain as large peripheral economies.

Chapter 5

One market, one money

Since the political decisions to begin Stage I, much research has been done to assess the pros and cons of EMU. The principal contribution was the Commission's study, 'One Market, One Money' (Commission of the European Communities 1990) and the associated academic papers (Commission 1991). Despite the subsequent change in the economic environment, this major study remains the *locus classicus* of the economic case for EMU, and provides a good framework for a review of the latest empirical work. After a brief summary of the major arguments, this chapter focuses mainly on the *benefits* of EMU, while Chapter 6 looks further at the *costs* and offers a conclusion.

Summary of benefits and costs

The Commission set out to examine the implications of moving from Stage I to the full-scale EMU of Stage III. The base case was taken to be completion of the Single Market legislation and consolidation of the ERM, involving participation in the narrow band by all Member States (or so it was hoped); the end case was EMU comprising a monetary union *with a single currency* and an economic union possessing 'a minimum of competences' involving common policies or coordination at the Community level, which might evolve over time (Commission 1990, p. 17).

Six major effects from EMU were identified. There were five main categories of *direct* benefits:

(1) elimination of *nominal exchange-rate variability and uncertainty*; this would reduce hedging costs and permit *lower real interest rates;*

(2) savings in *currency conversion and other transactions costs*;
(3) improvements in *transparency of prices*;
(4) establishment of *price stability* by more concerted and credible monetary policy; and
(5) development of the *European currency as a global transactions and investment medium.*

Three of the above categories – savings in transactions costs, improvements in price transparency and the global functions – would require a single currency, but the others would not necessarily do so. Other direct benefits were mentioned by the Commission but they are essentially subsidiary aspects of these main effects. It should be stressed that these are the 'direct' (i.e. immediate or *static*) consequences of EMU. There would also be *dynamic* effects which the Commission believed would be ultimately more important, as will be seen.

Against these benefits there might be important costs from:

(6) *losing the exchange rate as an adjustment mechanism.*

Whether or not these costs turn out to be major would depend on the nature and extent of disturbances affecting Member States and the effectiveness of other policies in securing adjustment, particularly fiscal policy.

Orders of magnitude were attached to some of these effects, although not all. Benefits from the elimination of *nominal exchange-rate uncertainty* were expected to be substantial in the long run, although not easy to quantify. The direct effects on GDP from lower foreign-exchange hedging costs would actually be quite be small (see below) but, more importantly, EMU would eliminate the risk premia in interest rates due to exchange-rate uncertainty experienced by most currencies in the ERM, even those within the narrow band. This would mean lower real interest rates for all but the anchor economy, Germany. There would be gains too from lower nominal interest rates, assuming that EMU would mean lower average inflation in the EC as a whole. Although the static impact on Community GDP would be modest, the long-run dynamic benefit from eliminating risk premia and from savings in transactions costs, through inducing more investment and raising productivity, could eventually be in excess of five percentage points on the level of GDP (see also below).

The direct benefit from savings in *intra-EC transactions costs* from the single currency was also expected to be fairly modest. Savings would be mainly 'financial', comprising the disappearance of the exchange margin and commission fees paid to banks, but would also include reductions in firms' in-house costs of currency management. The annual savings were put at 0.3–0.4% of GDP (ECU 20 to 25 billion per year at 1995 prices) for the Community as a whole, the bulk of which would be the financial component. Countries with small, open economies or weak or little-used currencies would save proportionately more – perhaps 1% of GDP on average. Within countries, the main gainers would be small and medium-sized firms, for which the cost of cross-border transactions is disproportionately high.

The benefits from *achieving and maintaining price stability* were expected to be large, but hard to quantify. The establishment of an independent central bank with a clear mandate to secure price stability would be instrumental in reducing inflation to that of the best-performing States, and doing so at lower costs to activity than is possible under existing regimes. This would work via the effect on inflation expectations of the policy credibility acquired through the strong political commitment to EMU. Price stability would confer long-run benefits through lower unemployment and higher per capita incomes.

The benefits from the development of *the single currency as an 'international vehicular currency'* were also hard to quantify, but some estimates were offered. EC trading firms would benefit from being able to do more of their business in their own currency. There would be modest seigniorage gains from the use of ECU banknotes in other countries. Foreign holdings of ECU-denominated assets would rise, but since they would incur market-related interest rates they would represent little net gain to the EC. The Community would be able to economize on its holdings of external reserve assets. Finally, EMU would 'unify and strengthen the Community's presence in international forums' like the G-7, and this would facilitate policy coordination at the global level. In the longer run, 'EMU could be a decisive building block for establishing a balanced tripolar monetary regime' (Commission 1990, p. 25).

Although it was accepted that the *loss of the exchange rate as an adjustment mechanism* could entail significant costs for some States, the Commission argued that they would be mainly transitional and should not be exaggerated. The Community's external exchange rate against the rest of the world would still be flexible, and would offer some scope for adjustment. ERM participants had already largely forgone the exchange rate as an adjustment mechanism (a contention subsequently, of course, disproved for non-core States), and even those outside were pursuing firm exchange-rate policies for counter-inflation reasons. Moreover changes in nominal exchange rates had been no ultimate guide to real exchange-rate changes (i.e. competitiveness) in the last decade; they had served only to offset differences in inflation. They could help to protect employment temporarily from adverse shocks, but only at the cost of higher inflation, and the employment gains disappeared eventually. Some real-exchange-rate changes would remain possible under EMU, because some prices (e.g. real estate) and wage costs, particularly in sectors sheltered from trade, could still change. Finally, EMU would confer an offsetting benefit in that conventional balance-of-payments constraints would disappear at the national level.

Since many of these effects could not be measured precisely, the Commission admitted that 'an overall quantitative asssessment of EMU would be meaningless' (p. 31). Nevertheless, their main conclusion was strong: 'On these grounds the economic case becomes strongly advantageous. Political union objectives may further be added. But the case can stand powerfully on economic criteria alone' (p. 29).

On the timing of effects, the key point was that the benefits were mainly long-term, whereas the costs were primarily short-term, likely to be most acute during transition; indeed for narrow-band ERM participants the costs of stabilizing exchange rates had already largely been absorbed, and a majority of States were already satisfactorily converged on inflation. Partly on this account, partly because imminent deadlines would help others to summon the political will to face the short-term costs, and partly because of possible exchange-rate instability in the transition, Stage II should be 'short'.

Exchange-rate variability and uncertainty

Although exchange-rate variability is much disliked by industrialists, as repeatedly shown by opinion surveys, the economic literature does not demonstrate convincingly that variability *per se* entails significant costs. Theory suggests that risk-averse agents will reduce their activity if there is variability in the expected rate of return, and the lags between contracting and payment in international trade are a common source of risk if exchange rates are flexible. On this view exchange-rate uncertainty tends to reduce international trade. However, some economists challenge the conventional view. For example Bliss (1994, Chapter 8) points out that exchange-rate uncertainty may actually increase some kinds of trade – because under imperfect competition, exchange-rate fluctuations around a stable level tend to raise average export profitability and this should

41

stimulate investment in export capacity by risk-inclined firms; while risk-averse firms may diversify their input sources in the face of currency uncertainty, which could increase trade. Theory also accepts that where there are developed financial markets traders can cover themselves through forward and futures transactions in foreign exchange. For straightforward short-period transactions the costs are modest – roughly equivalent to buying/selling spreads in the spot market. In more complex transactions, e.g. those involving options, the insurance costs are much greater, and hedging is difficult if not impossible over longer periods, because the markets for forward cover on maturities over one year are thin and costly. Accordingly *a priori* generalizations on this subject are hazardous.

The empirical evidence, which relates almost exclusively to high-frequency variability where hedging is efficient, is inconclusive, as the Commission admit (Commission 1990, p. 73). Although a few studies suggest small negative effects, they refer to bilateral situations which may not be typical, or to experience with the major floating currencies. In general, econometric work finds no systematic link between such variability and the volume of international trade.[1]

As one measure of the direct benefits from eliminating exchange-rate uncertainty, the Commission propose the savings in total costs (direct and indirect) of all intra-EC hedging operations incurred by firms, on the ground that irrevocable fixing of exchange rates amounts to free unlimited hedging for all trade and capital transactions. The resulting figure was too small to be quoted when scaled by GDP. As an additional and more substantial measure they suggested the average interest-rate differential between the narrow-band ERM currencies and the D-mark. The average saving was put at the equivalent of around ½% in the Community's real interest rate. The implied *direct* welfare gain from the latter would be very small – perhaps only around 0.05% of Community GDP, on the basis of one study (Commission 1990, p. 75) – but the *dynamic* effects via extra investment could be much larger (see below).

The Commission's estimates of direct benefits in this area were modest partly because they looked only at high-frequency variability and partly because the basis for comparison was taken to be the stable narrow-band ERM. Both these points are important. Although high-frequency variability may be a problem for small firms with little financial market expertise or suspect credit ratings, the kind of uncertainty which most businessmen complain about relates to real-exchange-rate swings in the medium term – perhaps five years, the horizon for much fixed investment and product or market development, too long to be covered by normal hedging operations.[2] Locking nominal exchange rates may not reduce this problem: although stable nominal rates usually mean stable real rates in the short term, because price and wage levels are comparatively sluggish, they will not necessarily mean real stability in the longer term, for EMU might not eradicate long-run changes in relative price or wages between States. Moreover stable real exchange rates may not always be welcome; they may be disadvantageous if the Community is hit by asymmetric shocks, or has not fully converged in its cost structure. Thus efficiency gains from elimination of longer-term *nominal*-exchange-rate uncertainty can be attributed with confidence to EMU only if it can be guaranteed that inflation convergence will be sustained in the long term. The Commission were probably right to be cautious in claiming benefits for EMU from eliminating 'low frequency' exchange-rate uncertainty.

Adoption of the narrow-band ERM as the basis for comparison meant leaving gains from eliminating premia on higher-risk currencies out of account – on the ground that such gains would be achieved by consolidation of the narrow-band ERM and are therefore not attributable to EMU, although this is not stated explicitly. The upsets seen in the ERM in 1992–3, and the renewed currency turbulence in the spring of 1995, inevitably call this comparison into question. Some economists believe with hindsight that it greatly understates the potential benefits from EMU, and is no longer appropriate (Thygesen 1993). In retrospect the Commission's vision of a tightly knit ERM with low currency-risk premia probably led them to an unduly conservative result here, and rather higher premia for all except the guilder and the schilling would be more appropriate for evaluating EMU effects. Such premia cannot of course be directly observed, but by making rough allowance for predictable *ex ante* inflation differentials it can be conjectured that an average premium of 1–1.5% p.a. for the EC as a whole is at stake; much more for some countries (Greece, Italy, Sweden) and less for others (Benelux, UK, France). This would imply significantly larger *static* gains from elimination of exchange-rate uncertainty than the Commission originally put forward.

Transactions costs

The Commission claim that their modest estimate for savings in transactions costs is conservative, partly on the ground that they are direct costs only, and do not include costs arising from the fragmentation of markets due to the implicit tax on cross-border business. Although economists have not challenged this estimate, or the notion that trans-actions costs may have wider effects, there are practical grounds for thinking it may be on the high side (as an estimate of direct savings).

The main reservation is that the estimated savings include costs of transferring funds between different *countries* as well as between *curren-cies*. The fact that bank charges for transfers of small sums are much larger than for Eurocheques suggests that the former include a large cost component reflecting the method of payment rather than mere currency conversion. At the corporate and wholesale level, the only transactions cost which relates solely to currency conversion is the exchange-rate spread; associated fees and commissions include payment for cross-border operations which would not disappear under a single currency. Significant improvements in the costs and timing of cross-border settle-ments are to be expected in Europe as the banking system becomes more integrated and better links are constructed between national payments systems, and smaller firms will benefit considerably from this. No doubt the prospect of EMU is helping to motivate these improvements, but the Single Market is probably a much stronger incentive – as demonstrated by the progress already being made in the settlements area, even with the single currency still a long way off, and doubtful in some States.

The Commission also probably exaggerate the in-house savings on currency management attributable to the single currency. Such opera-tions are often profitable for large sophisticated firms even where they deal largely in their own currencies, as US experience attests. Even after EMU some intra-EC trade will still be conducted in foreign currencies (oil, aircraft), as will some intra-EC transactions in financial and com-modity markets.

Transparency of prices

The Commission refer to a related type of benefit from the single currency, namely *information gains*. They cite the existence of price discrepancies for similar goods in different Member States, amounting in some cases to 100% or more, even where there are no formal trade barriers. Economists recognize the contribution that price transparency can make to economic efficiency and some believe that the information gains from a single currency would be a substantial benefit from EMU (Thygesen 1993). However although the former point may be valid, the latter seems debatable. A single currency would certainly improve price transparency, but it seems doubtful that the effect would be large in relation to the stimulus coming from the Single Market. Price discrepancies in Community trade are attributable mainly to transport costs and differences in consumer tastes, language and other cultural barriers, and over time they will be eroded by Single Market pressures. Home-currency prices of goods in competitive EU centres are available from mail-order services, trade catalogues, advertisements, consumers' associations and similar bodies. It is hard to accept that exchange rates *in themselves* comprise a significant information barrier.

Costs of introducing the single currency

The Commission dismiss the *costs of introducing the single currency* as 'small' relative to the efficiency gains, on the ground that they would be once-for-all, but this looks to have been over-optimistic. Recent surveys by the major banking associations suggest that currency conversion will present banks with difficult logistical problems and the costs will not be insignificant.[3] There will be sizeable costs in relation to changing the currency itself – minting coin and printing notes, storing and issuing them and withdrawing the old currency; machine conversion or replacement; amendments to banks' computer systems, including customer databases, accounting systems, card systems, etc.; and wider commercial costs to banks in particular, including the diversion of management time from profitable operations. Estimates now emerging suggest that the actual conversion would take three to four years, not counting prior investigation and planning; and the entire process of investigation, planning and conversion could take at least five years, perhaps longer.[4] The costs to the largest European banks have been put in the region of ECU 100–150 million each, or around 2% p.a. of operating costs for three years, assuming a 'big bang' conversion after careful preparation. This would imply direct costs for all EU banks of the order of ECU 8–10 billion (for UK banks, nearly £1 billion). The costs to the banks of a more protracted changeover involving dual-currency operations, although less disruptive for the public at large, could be 50% higher. In addition industrial and commercial firms would incur costs of redenominating financial and physical assets (inventories), adapting payment- and cash-handling systems, redenominating management, statutory and shareholder accounts, and converting all their financial systems, manual and computer-based. These could be particularly significant for retailers with extensive cash-handling systems, especially if there is a period of dual-currency running. Finally the public sector would incur costs of producing the new currency, educating the public, etc., while the public itself would experience considerable learning costs. The total income stream if invested in profitable alternatives would not be negligible.

Dynamic benefits

Although the orders of magnitude for static benefits in 'One Market, One Money' were mainly quite modest, the Commission argued that they would plausibly translate into 'a significant growth bonus from EMU' in the longer run (Commission 1990, p. 84). Longer-term gains were envisaged from two main sources. First, the central estimate of static efficiency gains from implementation of the Single Market, as presented in the Cecchini Report (Commission 1988), plus the saving in transactions and hedging costs, would be equivalent to almost 5% of GDP annually. Using a 'medium term growth multiplier' with a central value of two, the increase in GDP could accumulate to almost 10% in the longer run (after about ten years). The growth multipliers were taken from studies by Baldwin, on whose work the Commission rely heavily for their estimates of dynamic effects. Their size is somewhat conjectural, the methodology on which they are based being subject to certain criticisms.[5]

However, there is a more important weakness in the Commission's argument here: gains attributed to completion of the Single Market should not be included in an assessment of EMU which takes completion of Stage I as the comparative case. Had only the benefits from the reduction in currency conversion and hedging costs (i.e. those genuinely attributable to EMU) been counted, the medium-term increase in GDP would have been less than 1% (assuming a growth multiplier of two).

The Commission's second main source of long-term gains, the reduction in the cost of capital reflecting the elimination of the exchange-risk premium, put at around half a percentage point per annum for the EC as a whole, appears reasonable if the comparison is with the stable narrow-band ERM. The interest differential between the guilder and the D-mark, both low-inflation currencies, has tended to be of this order of magnitude since the early years of the ERM when the Dutch authorities established a close link to the D-mark. Following Baldwin, the Commission suggest that the associated improvement in the risk-adjusted rate of return to investment would raise Community GDP by 5–10% in the longer run (Commission 1990, p. 83). The argument is that a 0.5% decrease in the risk premium would raise the risk-adjusted return in the proportion of 5–10%, assuming that the EC's risk-adjusted rate of return lies between

5% and 10%; this should raise GDP in roughly the same proportion, assuming growth multipliers of between one and two. Even apart from doubts about the multipliers, this estimate seems on the high side. It is questionable whether the average investment response across the Community would be so large: much public-sector investment is not motivated by market-based rates of return, and not all private-sector investment is risk-averse. On the other hand, an estimate of this magnitude would be plausible if the case taken for comparison were not the stable narrow-band ERM but the more flexible system in place after August 1993. On that comparison, assuming EC average risk premia of the order of 1–1.5% p.a., the *direct* benefits from removing exchange-rate uncertainty would be correspondingly greater than the Commission suggested, and the longer-run effects perhaps not very different at around 5% of GDP (assuming a smaller investment response and lower growth multipliers).[6]

Price stability

The potential gains from price stability are among the most important benefits claimed for EMU but the most difficult to assess. There are three key issues: the benefits from eliminating inflation, and associated costs; the contribution that independent central banks can make to price stability; and whether the proposed central bank of EMU can achieve price stability more effectively than national monetary regimes, most of which are moving towards independence.

Effects of inflation

The Commission rightly stress the importance of distinguishing between anticipated and unanticipated inflation, the latter entailing much larger costs. They seem on safe ground in believing the microeconomic effects of *anticipated* inflation to be fairly modest – the loss of welfare that occurs when inflation raises the private opportunity cost of holding money (i.e. the interest rate on risk-free financial assets), implying increased transactions costs for people and firms as they finance expenditure with reduced real-money balances; and the accompanying 'menu' costs and inflation tax (Commission 1990, p. 88 and Chapter 2). They cite empirical work based on conventional demand for money functions which suggests that the welfare loss from suboptimal money holdings associated with inflation might be around 0.3% of Community GDP, if the relevant money stock is M1 ('narrow money', i.e. cash and sight deposits). That estimate is probably on the high side, since some sight deposits in the Community now carry market-related interest rates and since trend inflation is now well below the illustrative rate of 10% used in the study. On menu costs (the costs of continually having to update price lists) the Commission concede that the direct costs are likely to be negligible, and although some economists are beginning to suggest there may be significant wider effects on output and prices, no quantitative estimates have yet been made.

The macroeconomic costs of *anticipated* inflation were also assessed as modest, since the traditional Phillips-curve relation between inflation and unemployment no longer holds in the long run, essentially because agents have learned to anticipate inflation (on the argument of Chapter 4 above). The Commission refer to the 'large body' of empirical literature which suggests there is no stable trade-off between inflation and unemployment and refer to data for OECD countries which show that over a 15-year period to 1985 average unemployment was *positively* correlated with average inflation; and that there was no correlation between growth of per capita GDP and inflation among OECD countries over a 30-year period. They also note that high inflation tends to be unstable, and present data for OECD countries showing a positive correlation between inflation and its variability: if inflation is high on average it becomes less predictable.

It is widely accepted that *unanticipated* inflation has strong microeconomic effects via the 'surprise' inflation tax (because much government debt carries fixed nominal interest rates and tax systems are mainly non-indexed), but the Commission offer no quantification; and also via higher variability of relative prices, on which they cite Cukierman's survey (1983). Estimates for Germany are referred to which suggest that a one per cent increase in the variability of relative prices lowers potential output by some 0.3% (Neumann and von Hagen 1991). Unanticipated inflation may also mean significant macroeconomic costs, and here the Commission stress the loss of policy credibility when governments are tempted to take advantage of the short-term Phillips-curve trade-off. The problems of estimating these costs are severe, because the wage behaviour which determines the 'sacrifice ratio' (the output loss per unit of reduction in inflation achieved by deflationary policies) varies with national circumstances, as may the policy regime. It was strongly contended that these costs would be lower under EMU, but no quantitative estimates were offered, and it was admitted that the evidence for behavioural changes among wage and price setters under the EMS was weak.

The Commission's analysis of inflation effects is largely in tune with latest mainstream economic thinking. Although others' research suggests different results in some areas, the general consensus is that growth is significantly and negatively correlated with inflation.[7] In one recent exercise, Fischer assembles a list of direct economic costs from inflation, anticipated and unanticipated, in industrial economies and arrives at a figure of 2–5% of GNP for 10% inflation (Fischer 1994, p. 17). He agrees that the welfare gain from eliminating transactions costs of inflation in the G7 countries is likely to be small, but suggests that inflation-based distortions in tax systems are important, mainly because they discourage capital accumulation, and these could 'easily have a social cost amounting to 2–3% of GNP at an inflation rate of 10 per cent' (p. 14). He also cites research which suggests that the disincentive effects on both physical and financial investment from variability in relative prices and inflation uncertainty (positively correlated with inflation) are appreciable, while pointing out that they could be reduced by indexation.

Fischer also refers to his own econometric evidence on the long-term relationship between growth and inflation, which comes out as significantly negative (Fischer 1993), but he concedes that the direction of causality is not well established: if high inflation is caused by negative supply shocks, then the negative correlation may simply reflect the common impact of such shocks; or some of the correlation may just reflect cyclical factors, i.e. that productivity growth is low near the peak of the cycle, when inflation pressures are high, a result that seems to be borne out for OECD countries. Thus although the latest empirical work tends to support a negative long-run relation between output growth and inflation among a large sample of countries, it is less firmly established among mature industrial economies (as the Commission admitted) and there are unresolved questions about causality.

Central-bank independence

The view that independent central banks have a better record on inflation – because they give priority to reducing inflation and are less subject to political pressures than elected governments – has received increasing attention from economists in recent years. The Commission argue that these two features are indispensable for a stable and credible monetary regime, insisting that central banks must be relieved of the responsibility of financing government borrowing and the temptation to resort to inflation to reduce the real government debt. They refer for empirical support to work by Alesina (1989) which found a negative relationship

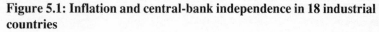

Figure 5.1: Inflation and central-bank independence in 18 industrial countries

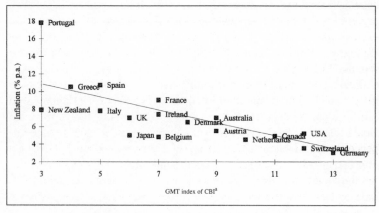

Source: Fischer (1994), Figure 6.

[a] Index of central-banking independence compiled by Grilli, Masciandaro and Tabellini (1991).

between average inflation and an index of central-bank independence among some 17 industrial countries, 1973–86.

More recent econometric work gives qualified support to this finding. Eijffinger and Schaling (1993) find a negative correlation between inflation variability and central-banking independence using one index of central-banking independence, but not on three others, and they find no link at all between output variability and central-banking independence. Fischer (1994, p. 44) reports a significant negative relationship between inflation and independence for 18 industrial countries over the period 1960–92 (illustrated here in Figure 5.1). But a relationship of this kind does not appear to hold when extended to a much larger sample including non-industrial countries (Cukierman et al. 1992).

Although the evidence appears to support a negative link between inflation and central-banking independence among industrial countries, caution is needed. First, it is questionable how well the indices capture independence in practice; some do not correlate well with inflation. This is hardly surprising, given the arbitrariness of the weighting schemes and values attributed to legal characteristics, and the fact that in many regimes the legal provisions do not accurately reflect the central bank's actual exercise of autonomy. Secondly, the apparent negative relationship owes a lot to a few relatively extreme observations, as can be seen in Figure 5.1. Thirdly, there is a possibility of reverse causality, or common dependence on third factors. A plausible inference is that low inflation and high central-bank independence are both symptoms of social 'tastes' – public preference for low inflation, as exemplified most notably in Germany, reflecting the collective memory of the damage done by high inflation there in the interwar period.

Two other findings from this research seem relevant. First, there appears to be no clear link from central-banking independence to output growth (Grilli, Masciandaro and Tabellini 1991; Alesina and Summers 1988: Cukierman et al. 1993). This is sometimes cited as evidence that independence does not detract from growth, but it also implies that it does not improve growth either. Secondly, independence does not appear to improve the sacrifice ratio; indeed on Fischer's evidence, it worsens it: independent central banks on average pay a *higher* output price per percentage point of inflation to reduce the inflation rate. Fischer comments that this 'suggests that there is no credibility bonus in the labor markets for more independent central banks: they have to prove their toughness repeatedly, by being tough' (Fischer 1994, p. 50). Other research tends to confirm this finding, and there is some suggestion that higher central-bank independence may actually increase nominal wage and price rigidities, by reducing agents' expectations of nominal shocks (Briault 1995). For those who maintain that independent central banks minimize the costs of securing low inflation, this is an awkward result, implying that independence works less by reducing the costs of price stability than by making anti-inflation policy less subject to political pressure.

EMU versus national regimes

There is finally the issue of the relative merits of EMU and national monetary regimes for securing price stability. Economists are perhaps not best placed to assess this issue, although several have written about it; the questions are essentially political and legal, rather than economic. The advantages for European policy-makers of tying their hands to an external policy regime were much debated in the context of the EMS (for example by Giavazzi and Pagano 1988). The claim for EMU in comparison with the stable or 'hard' ERM rests on the additional strength of the Treaty commitment and of the new bank's constitution (Corden 1993; Currie 1992; among others). Experience has shown that commitments under the ERM are by no means sacrosanct: where national economic interests are at stake, currencies can realign or leave the system. That would be more difficult under EMU, although not impossible. However, as the Commission (1990, p. 98) and economists (Krugman 1990) have pointed out, pressures could arise within EMU from time to time which could divert the central bank from its strict objective – even to the extent of making it less effective in pursuit of price stability than the stable ERM. Whether they will do so will depend in part on the precise provisions written into the new bank's constitution. Total absence in EMU's early years of any track record on which 'reputation' could rest would be an important drawback. These questions will be returned to in Chapter 8.

The international dimension

The benefits from the development of the single currency as a major world currency would include savings in transactions and hedging costs like those identified at the intra-EC level, but in this case arising from the use of the new ECU in transactions with non-EC residents. First, there would be small savings in transactions costs equivalent to up to 0.05% of Community GDP (Commission 1990, p. 183), and there would also be small gains from reducing exchange risks through ECU invoicing, and by enabling European banks to do more business in their own currencies (fewer risk exposures to hedge, increased transactions balances held in ECU). Secondly there would be gains from economies in external foreign-exchange reserve-holding by Member States' monetary authorities, but the benefit would be modest since it would reflect only the difference between what these resources would earn if invested in alternative uses and what they already earn in interest. Thirdly there would be 'seigniorage' benefits from additional holdings of ECUs as official reserves by external monetary authorities (mainly in central and eastern Europe). These would also be very modest, because interest would have to be paid on them. More significant seigniorage benefits would arise from enlarged holdings of non-interest-bearing ECU notes by private agents outside the Community. A stock adjustment of some $35 billion was foreseen, the interest savings on which would imply an addition to Community GDP of less than 0.05% (p. 186). Fourthly, it was envisaged that the emergence of the new ECU as a major trading currency would lead to some increase of demand for EC currency-denominated assets in financial markets. Again, the effect would probably be small, because portfolios of private international investing institutions are already relatively well diversified and because there would be some reduction in demand for individual States' currencies for hedging purposes. The total shift was put at around 5% of existing portfolios, which would be in the nature of a stock adjustment lasting several years (p. 188). No precise estimate of dynamic effects was possible, but it was argued that the implied temporary increase in the flow of ECU assets supplied to non-residents might be accompanied by some appreciation of the ECU exchange rate, which would in turn imply some temporary increase in EC net imports of goods and services (preferably investment goods); alternatively or as well, there could be a temporary increase in EC net direct investment or portfolio/bank lending externally.

Although these assessments are inevitably somewhat speculative, most economists would probably endorse the general conclusion that the scale of the direct external gains will be modest. An appreciable share of EC external trade may continue to be transacted in dollars, and the ECU's external exchange rate would still be subject to uncertainty. D-mark-denominated securities are already available for risk-averse investors seeking to hedge against inflation. The hysteresis effects in international currency usage are quite strong, and there has already been a drift away from the dollar towards European currencies as well as the yen in international payments, reserve holding and international bond markets in the 1980s, as Alogoskoufis and Portes (1991) stress. In their view the ECU of EMU is likely to become the dominant payments and unit of account currency within Europe and its periphery, but is unlikely to make inroads into the American and Pacific regions. Even so, the Commission may rather understate the extent to which a single currency with good price stability credentials would in time boost the demand for European hard-currency assets in those regions. And they appear to overlook the possibility of significant redistributive effects within EMU, if (for example) weaker-currency States receive capital inflows as third-country investors diversify from predominantly D-mark-denominated bonds into other single-currency assets in due course.

The alleged *international policy gains* from EMU are more controversial and economists, other than those writing on the continent, have mainly been sceptical. The essence of the Commission's argument is that the benefits from policy coordination will increase and the EU will acquire greater bargaining power in discussions at G-7 level, because the spillover effects of EC policies on the US economy will be perceived to be greater under EMU than now. However, this assumes that the Community would speak and act with one voice in G-7 discussions whereas, as Kenen (1992) and Goodhart (1992b) have argued, this is far from assured. A counterargument is that strategic decisions on exchange-rate policy and other policies will remain in ministerial hands after EMU. Consultation with the ECB on matters affecting monetary policy will no doubt take place (and is required under the Treaty), and the ECOFIN Council will collectively negotiate on international monetary and foreign-exchange matters (*Treaty*, Article 109.3). But the same Article (109.5) says that Member States may negotiate in international bodies without prejudice to Community competence on EMU – which implies that national finance ministers would attend G-7 meetings to discuss fiscal or other non-monetary policy matters.

As Williamson (1992) has pointed out, central bankers might be more influential in G-7 meetings if there were four of them instead of seven, but he doubts whether the replacement of the D-mark by the ECU as the world's third key currency would make it easier for the G-7 to adopt target zones for exchange rates or demand growth. Only if experience under EMU persuades EU governments in due course of the advantages of cooperation across a wider spectrum of economic policies will the Commission's more ambitious claims in this sphere begin to be borne out.

Chapter 6

Adjusting without the exchange rate

Most economists would agree that there are important risks in abandoning the exchange rate as an adjustment mechanism and, along with it, the ability to pursue an independent monetary policy. This chapter reviews the findings of the Commission and other researchers on this set of issues, and offers overall conclusions on the economic case for EMU.

Shocks under EMU

The Commission accept that the Community is subject to both symmetric and asymmetric shocks but believe that it is relatively resilient in the face of the latter, owing to the advanced state of industrial integration among the core States (Commission of the European Communities 1990, p. 142).[1] Completion of the Single Market will mean further integration and EMU should also help by eliminating shocks from volatility of (intra-EC) exchange rates and aberrant national monetary policies.

This view seems overly sanguine in several respects. First, as seen in Chapter 4, the peripheral economies are less integrated than the core, and this disparity seems bound to grow as the EU expands. Secondly, economic integration may ultimately promote industrial specialization, as Krugman observed for the USA, and this could make shocks less uniform in their effects. Thirdly, experience of shocks may not repeat itself. The Community has been subject over the past two decades to at least four major unexpected shocks which have had important asymmetric effects – the two oil-price shocks, the US-led interest-rate hike at the end of the 1970s and German reunification. It is hard to predict what other major upsets are in store, but there probably will be some.

Fourthly, a new type of asymmetry may develop under EMU with a single monetary policy, reflecting differences between the monetary transmission mechanisms of EC economies, as Crockett (1994, p. 182) among others has pointed out. These arise from differences in financial structures and practices, for example levels of credit utilization by the household sector, and shares of fixed and variable-rate borrowing in mortgage, company and government finance (Easton and Stephenson 1990). Accordingly a given change in short-term interest rates will have larger effects in an economy like the UK's with deregulated and highly competitive financial markets than in continental economies, where the main lending rates are sluggish, there is more fixed-rate finance, and households are less heavily geared. If an otherwise symmetric shock (e.g. an increase in global demand for EC exports) were met by a uniform increase in money-market interest rates, the impact on domestic demand in the UK would be substantially larger than in France or Germany. In due course, developing competition in the Single Financial Area will probably narrow these discrepancies, but the process could easily take a decade or more; and discrepancies which are due to differences in national tax and regulatory systems may persist longer.

Is devaluation an effective remedy?

While conceding that asymmetric shocks matter to some extent in the Community, the Commission argue that devaluation is not an effective way of coping with them, because of real-wage rigidities. The arguments are familiar: initially output benefits from devaluation after an adverse external shock, but it takes longer to re-establish equilibrium because necessary downward adjustment to real wages is delayed and the process leaves an inflation legacy. Reference is made to results of standard macroeconomic model simulations for the major economies which suggest that most of the stimulative effects of a devaluation on output disappear after about five years (Commission 1990, p. 139). It is also argued that devaluation is not a solution to structural problems such as unequal rates of productivity growth; there is only weak evidence of correlation between Member States' long-term growth rates and trends in either real or nominal exchange rates.

These views also deserve qualification. The reported model simulations take no account of the policy regime or the state of the economy. Devaluation may be more effective if it occurs when economic activity is depressed or when the authorities have established credibility in their anti-inflation stance, as illustrated by the subdued inflation response seen in the UK and Italy after the sharp depreciations that accompanied their departure from the ERM in September 1992; in both cases, the sluggishness of the inflation response owes a lot to the aftermath of recession. More fundamentally, the Commission appear to confuse the active use of the exchange rate as a policy instrument with its market-driven role as an adjustment mechanism. EC experience over the past two decades clearly shows that real exchange rates can diverge from sustainable levels for quite long periods under quasi-fixed exchange rates (as will be illustrated in the next chapter), but ultimately markets perceive the problem and force a nominal rate adjustment which returns relative costs to near sustainable levels. Countries with low-trend productivity growth seem rather prone to this pattern, and without such adjustment might need periodic phases of high unemployment to restore long-run balance. Preferably, their real wages should be more flexible and their productivity growth nearer the Community average, but the exchange rate is not an ineffective safety valve in the circumstances.

Finally it should be borne in mind that monetary policy can affect the economy other than via the exchange rate. The responsiveness of expenditure and saving to interest rates appears small in the core economies which have chosen to link their currencies to the D-mark, but there are still significant domestic effects in economies with flexible exchange rates, which retain some scope to use interest rates independently. Even in a world of mobile international capital movements, monetary policy is still a useful instrument for managing demand, if nowadays more with the aim of stabilizing prices than activity. Some economists fear that by removing that instrument EMU may pose serious problems:

> The main cost, that is perceived for EC states, is the abandonment by national authorities of a major instrument of demand management, the use of monetary policy. Interest rates and exchange rates are key prices within any economy. (Goodhart 1993, p. 15)

Similar worries have been expressed by others (for example David Begg 1991). The impact of interest rates on domestic expenditure has actually grown in the UK economy with financial liberalization since the late 1970s (Easton and Stephenson 1990) and similar changes may happen in other EC economies as liberalization proceeds there too. This gap in the Commission's approach means that they tend to underplay the contribution that an independent monetary policy can make in economies outside the ERM core.

Wage flexibility

Since exchange-rate adjustment will not be possible within EMU, shocks and adverse cost trends will have to be alleviated in other ways. The Commission accept that labour mobility is unlikely to improve much, even when formal barriers are removed under the Single Market legislation; and they concede that real-wage rigidities in Europe are stronger than in the USA and Japan (on evidence of the kind described in Chapter 4). Nevertheless they hope that wage flexibility will improve under EMU. They think this has already happened in the core States under the influence of ERM discipline but their evidence is not very convincing; for example, wage flexibility between regions of pre-unification Germany is very low (Commission 1990, Graph 6.7), owing to the operation of fiscal 'bailouts' among the German *Länder* and of national wage norms. Moreover the experience of upward wage equalization in former East Germany after reunification does not bode well for EMU; nor does the fact that any EMU grouping is likely to be collectively less open to external competition than the separate economies are now. Accordingly the Commission's optimism here is rightly cautious: wages should become more flexible as the Single Market induces greater industrial integration, and under the tougher competitive discipline of EMU, assuming no fiscal bailouts. On the other hand, the high profile given to 'social cohesion' under EMU may inhibit wider income differentials, and harmonization of labour standards under the EC's social policies might also work against wage flexibility.

Model simulations

In principle, econometric models that embody all the relevant relationships ought to be able to shed light on adjustment under alternative exchange-rate regimes. The Commission report an exercise using the IMF's Multimod model to explore the stability performance of four regimes (Commission 1990, pp. 152–7). Their conclusion was that, on the criterion of minimizing deviations in output and prices from baseline levels, the EMU regime with a single monetary policy outperformed its nearest rival, the 'asymmetric' ERM (in which all four EC majors adopt German monetary policy), which in turn outperformed the two other regimes – an adjustable ERM with an automatic realignment rule and fully floating exchange rates. These results are attributed to the dampening effect of lower inflation expectations on wage and price formation under fixed exchange rates; the elimination of futile competitive intra-Community exchange appreciations, which removes a source of inflation variability; and the removal of non-policy-induced exchange-rate shocks. The results are said to show that the EMU regime contains features which could compensate to an important extent for the loss of the exchange-rate instrument (Commission 1990, p. 155).

However, these results have been strongly challenged by other researchers. A corresponding exercise using the Liverpool world model reached diametrically opposite results (Minford, Rastogi and Hughes-Hallet 1992). They find that the best regime for EC countries would be floating, with policies preferably coordinated globally, or, failing that, coordinated within the EC, in a world of uncoordinated behaviour in which blocs anticipate one another's policy actions. In the absence of policy coordination, the UK would do best to stay out of EMU and float. Differences in the results appear to turn substantially on the methodological treatment of risk premia in the selection of the exchange-rate errors used in the stochastic simulations; that is, they largely reflect differences in the design of the exchange-rate experiments, rather than the model properties. This view is supported by the proprietors of the IMF model, who conducted a similar exercise to the Commission's but reached different conclusions (Masson and Symansky 1992): namely that although the EMS is less of a potential source of instability than Minford et al. suggest, EMU is not clearly superior to the other regimes. Comparing these three exercises, Barrell and Whitley (1992) find in favour of the fully model-consistent framework used by Minford et al. as against the random-walk method used by Masson and Symansky, and *a fortiori* against the Commission's approach.

Removal of the external-payments constraint

One compensation claimed by the Commission for the loss of the exchange rate as an adjustment mechanism under EMU is the removal of national balance-of-payments constraints. Where capital is internationally mobile, a country with a deficiency of domestic savings in relation to domestic investment is liable to run an external current-account deficit, financed by inward investment or borrowing from non-residents; but market-based financing depends on the deficit being perceived as

59

sustainable. Under EMU the conventional balance-of-payments constraint will not operate: capital will move freely across borders to finance investment projects, and the only limitation (the Commision argue) will come from long-run solvency constraints on companies, households and governments (Commission 1990, p. 162).

This argument seems highly questionable. There is a danger that if external deficits become invisible, more leeway will be provided for unsustainable national policies, for example fiscal policy (if EMU's fiscal constraints are not wholly effective – see below), and structural problems may be ignored. The absence of statistics showing a payments deficit would not of course remove underlying causes. If aggregate demand in an economy rises persistently faster than potential output, cost pressures will develop sooner or later, and in time the effect will show under EMU as a national profitability squeeze, falling domestic investment (including inward investment), and ultimately rising unemployment if the cost inflation is not corrected. Long-run solvency considerations are not the only motivation driving private investment; profitability is crucial for new investment in the short to medium term. Greater intra-EC capital mobility will accentuate, not attenuate, those mechanisms. Markets and governments should be aware of these dangers in EMU, and the latter may wish to continue collecting and publishing at least summary national balance-of-payments statistics. Private capital may flow more readily across national boundaries in EMU because of the elimination of exchange risk, but the constraints imposed by profitability considerations are unlikely to be relaxed much. EMU will certainly eliminate the very rapid and large movements of liquid funds that tend to precede, and sometimes precipitate, currency devaluations, and economists would naturally accept that as an important benefit.

Fiscal policy

The Commission foresee a greater onus falling on fiscal policy for preserving internal balance under EMU, given the existence of wage and price rigidities which enable fiscal instruments to affect domestic demand in the short term, although they see some risks in the longer term. In some respects fiscal policy will have greater domestic leverage under EMU, for when exchange rates are flexible, fiscal expansions tend to leak overseas, through exchange-rate appreciation associated with an increase in domestic interest rates; whereas under fixed exchange rates with capital mobility the latter effect is likely to be small domestically, and in the case of a dominant country upward pressure on interest rates is likely to be diluted by percolating abroad. In other respects, fiscal policy leverage may be smaller under EMU, either because the markets exact higher interest premia on fears of government insolvency, or because fiscal deficits are constrained by mandatory rules. For those reasons, fiscal policy is not seen as a solution to *permanent* shocks. EMU is nevertheless expected to be favourable on balance for fiscal stabilization, in part because the new regime will boost wage flexibility and thereby create greater scope for trade-off between short-term fiscal stabilization and the speed of wage and price adjustment (Commission 1990, p. 165).

Most economists would accept this general position; there is a large literature in support of the view that fiscal instruments have greater leverage in fixed-rate regimes, based on the influential Mundell-Fleming model (see, for example, Mundell 1963). However, there are two special concerns about EMU, which point to mutually conflicting conclusions. First, the removal of the exchange rate as a barometer of national fiscal prudence, together with the short-term balance-of-payments constraint, may encourage fiscal irresponsibility; and loss of seigniorage as a source of government revenue in some States may add to these incentives.[2] Against this, some commentators have argued that the capital markets will impose an effective discipline on governments through adding risk premia to interest charges where there are doubts about creditworthiness, and eventually by suspending lending where debt accumulation threatens to be unsustainable (Bishop et al. 1989). On this view, market discipline on governments should be enhanced under EMU, provided its 'no bail-out' rules are effective. (But there will be a penalty in that real interest rates incurred by heavily indebted governments will be higher than they would be if others were allowed to come to their rescue.) There is relevant experience in Canada, where the federal government has no obligation to come to the aid of financially distressed provinces. However, there are well-known cases in federal states where market discipline has not worked effectively – for example the New York City debt crisis in 1975 – and they feed doubts that market constraints on their own would suffice in the EU where central fiscal compensation machinery is on a small scale but political pressures for intergovernment bailouts can be strong. Such doubts could be countered to some extent by reforms that would make market discipline work better, for example in the area of prudential supervision, where tightening the capital adequacy and 'large exposure' rules might improve the efficiency of market lending to governments (Bishop 1991b). Nevertheless worries about possible fiscal

61

Table 6.1: Estimates of the degree of interregional income redistributions and regional stabilization in selected federal and unitary countries through central public-finance channels (%)

	Interregional redistribution		Regional stabilization	
USA	35-44	(Sachs and Sala-i-Martin 1989)	10	(Von Hagen 1992)[a]
	25	(MacDougall 1977)	28	(Bayoumi and Masson 1991)
			20	(Goodhart and Smith 1993)
			17	(Pisani-Ferry et al. 1993)
Canada	30	(MacDougall)	17	(Bayoumi and Masson)
			24	(Goodhart and Smith)
Germany	35	(MacDougall)	33-42	(Pisani-Ferry et al.)
Australia	50	(MacDougall)		
Switzerland	15[b]	(MacDougall)		
France	53	(MacDougall)	37	(Pisani-Ferry et al.)
UK	34	(MacDougall)	34	(Goodhart and Smith)

[a] Tax side only.
[b] Incomplete data.
Source: Commission of the European Communities (1993a).

imprudence were behind the adoption of rigid rules on fiscal deficits in the Treaty. While this was understandable in principle, the actual rules chosen could seriously limit the ability of national governments to pursue sensible fiscal policies, as argued by Buiter et al. (1993).

A second, related, concern arises from the absence of a central EC budget to assist fiscal stabilization. Some economists believe this could be a serious problem under EMU, when monetary policy will no longer be available for stabilization at the national level, and if, as cannot be ruled out, participating economies are subject to unsynchronized cycles or asymmetric shocks. Goodhart (1993) gives a number of reasons: the decreased effectiveness of national fiscal policies in an integrating EC (with larger spillovers); the absence of effective obligations or incentives for national governments to coordinate fiscal policies; the constraints on national action imposed by the Treaty's excessive-deficit procedure, particularly the 3% deficit–GDP ratio; and increasing factor mobility under EMU, which will make it difficult for national jurisdictions to pursue differential tax policies.

Much empirical work has been devoted to the interregional aspects of fiscal arrangements in existing federal states, particularly the USA. The first such study was undertaken by Sachs and Sala-i-Martin (1989), who concluded that the automatic fiscal stabilizers operating at the federal level in the USA compensate for some 35–44% of the effects of region-specific shocks to personal incomes. In contrast, no more than 1% of shocks to income in EC Member States are compensated by variations in EC taxes (Eichengreen 1990b). These results have been contested by von Hagen (1992), mainly on the ground that they relate to redistributive transfers rather than stabilization; he estimates the cushioning effect of the US federal budget on regional income changes at only 10%. Subsequent exercises have produced somewhat higher estimates of regional stabilization effects contributed by the fiscal arrangements of central government budgets in the USA and other countries (see Table 6.1).

Concerns of this kind have led to proposals for Community *stabilization* schemes which would operate through the central budget. The essential features of such schemes are that they would be automatic and rapid, and would cover only temporary asymmetric disturbances (Goodhart and Smith 1993). They should therefore work on the insurance principle and should not involve cumulative transfers between States. Italianer and Vanheukelen (1993) devised a scheme based on year-to-year changes in national unemployment rates relative to the Community average; they calculate on the basis of experience in the past decade that approximately the same degree of income stabilization as operates in the USA could be provided in the EC at an annual cost of as little as 0.2% of Community GDP. They attribute the smallness of their estimate to the fact that their scheme excludes redistribution and other social objectives, and argue that the risk of moral hazard or country bias should therefore also be small.

Others have disputed the value of such schemes, maintaining that their benefits are insignificant whereas the risks of moral hazard, through encouraging governments to pursue inappropriate policies, are large.[3] Moreover if the costs are so modest, stabilization can readily be achieved at the national level instead, as Masson and Melitz (1990) have shown for common shocks hitting the French and German economies – provided fiscal mechanisms are allowed to work fairly freely. However, it is not easy to reconcile such low estimates with the fact that most Member States' deficits are currently well in excess of 3% of GDP, owing partly to the operation of the automatic stabilizers in response to recession. Since much of the EC recession of the early 1990s was ultimately attributable to the (asymmetric) shock of German reunification and policy responses to it, it is hard to escape the conclusion that the budgetary implications of coping with large country-specific shocks in the Community may at times greatly exceed the deficit limits set in the Treaty.

Regional redistribution

It is important in the EMU debate to distinguish between fiscal stabilization and the role played by central public finance in regional income redistribution. Goodhart and Smith define as regional redistribution, variations in the levels of public expenditure and taxes that are functions of the *level* of economic activity (real or nominal incomes or employment); and as stabilization, expenditure and tax variations that are functions of the *rate of change* of economic activity (1993, pp. 419–20). The arguments for redistribution relate essentially to equity and social cohesion; those for stabilization, to economic efficiency (income smoothing in the face of market rigidities).

Table 6.1 showed that central budgets typically offset through taxes and transfer payments between a quarter and a half of regional disparities in average primary income levels within monetary unions. This is much more than the redistribution which occurs overall through the Community budget, although the importance of transfers to the poorest States is greater than commonly thought (Bini-Smaghi and Vori, who show that EC transfers to Ireland are as large per capita as federal transfers to the poorest US states; 1992, pp. 95–6). The Commission admit that the Community is different from existing federations, combining high fiscal autonomy with low fiscal equalization. While not proposing a radical change, they suggest (Commission 1990, p. 168) 'some recalibration' of the role of central public finance in the Community, to offset increases in

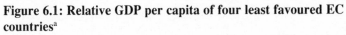

Figure 6.1: Relative GDP per capita of four least favoured EC countries[a]

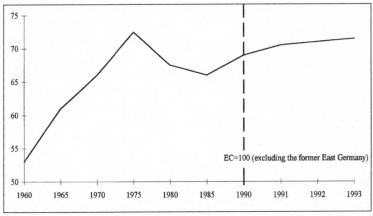

Source: Commission of the European Communities (1993a).

[a] Greece, Spain, Ireland and Portugal.

regional income disparities which EMU may well cause. They suspect that EMU may actually lead to reductions in the size of national public sectors, through decreases in seigniorage and revenue shrinkage from tax competition. The role of central finance could be enhanced through shock-absorption mechanisms (such as the insurance scheme mentioned above) or through increased structural funds for education, transport and housing which would help to improve adjustment capacities in the Community's poorer regions.

The likely regional implications of EMU are difficult to assess, as the Commission concede. After a marked initial reduction in the 1960s and early 1970s, there has been no clear trend in per capita income disparities between Member States; they have tended to narrow in periods of rapid growth and widen when growth slows (see Figure 6.1). Adjustment to the competitive pressures of the Single Market is likely to be felt more in the economies that are undergoing deep structural change – Greece, Portugal and Ireland and the poorer parts of Italy and Spain – which are benefiting from the doubling of structural funds in real terms from 1987 to 1993. These countries are also likely to be affected most by the fixing of exchange rates in EMU, because their adjustment costs will be sharper in transition.

65

Table 6.2: Disparities in per capita GDP in the European Communities (Index EC-12 = 100)

Country	Per capita GDP index		Highest region	Per capita GDP index		Lowest region	Per capita GDP index	
	1980	1989		1980	1989		1980	1989
Belgium	104	101	Antwerp	127	122	Hainaut	82	75
Denmark	108	107						
Germany/W.	114	112	Hamburg	179	173	Lüneburg	81	78
Greece	58	54	Sterea Ellada	80	69	Ipeiros	42	39
Spain	74	77	Baleares	90	104	Extremadura	47	49
France	112	109	Île de France	158	162	Corsica	n/a	79
Ireland	64	67						
Italy	102	104	Lombardy	135	139	Calabria	58	57
Luxembourg	118	129						
Netherlands	111	102	Noord-Holland	125	119	Flevoland	n/a	66
Portugal	55	55	Lisbon	71	70	Centro	44	45
UK	101	107	Southeast	119	131	N. Ireland	77	79

Note: No data are available for the new *Länder* in East Germany, the French overseas departments or the Portuguese Islands. In these countries, the missing regions would have lower GDPs than the regions shown. In the UK, the regional disaggregation is less than in other countries. In the Netherlands, the artificially high figure reported for Groningen has been disregarded here.

Source: Eurostat Rapid Report (1991), no. 2. Reproduced in Begg and Mayes (1992).

There are some grounds for thinking that in the very long run the peripheral regions should fare comparatively well under EMU. Economic integration will benefit the low-income countries by virtue of their low wage costs, which are attractive to international firms. Against that, economies of scale and transport costs may continue to draw industry to the central locations. The net effect of these opposing tendencies seems highly unclear. On the other hand, certain of the benefits that are specific to EMU should operate very favourably for the less developed economies in time: improvements in price stability, savings from lower transactions costs, and the reduction in real and nominal interest rates should all benefit the peripheral, higher-inflation economies most in due course.

Economic theory offers little clear guidance on the likely implications of currency areas for regional development. Economists of a neoclassical persuasion believe that monetary integration should help convergence of economic performance in the long run, on the basis that free trade should be mutually advantageous if there are different factor endowments or relative factor prices, and provided the terms of trade are free to adjust. However, the assumptions underlying this theory are fairly restrictive, in particular that production technologies are the same in all regions. A newer 'divergence' school sees technology as endogenous and stresses the externalities from spatial concentration of economic activity (Santos 1993). The implication from this literature is that regional growth rates may diverge under free trade, and the divergences may be accentuated by EMU.

Such questions can only be resolved by empirical research, but work on these topics is still in its infancy. Business-survey results suggest that although 'centripetal' forces are important in firms' location decisions, good local infrastructures and labour skills combined with lower wage costs are also attractive. Begg and Mayes (1992) draw attention to the exceptional size of regional income disparities in the Community (see Table 6.2); they are much larger than between the richest and poorest states in the USA (p. 223). Other studies confirm that regional per capita output disparities were appreciably lower in the USA in the 1960s and early 1970s than in the EC, and tended to fall, whereas they remained approximately constant in the EC. However, it is unclear how far the US pattern is due to monetary union, and how far to redistributive fiscal transfers, or to greater factor mobility.

It seems inevitable that the costs associated with *transition* to EMU will bear more heavily on the poorer States; they are industrially less integrated with the core, and therefore less likely to respond in the same way to common shocks; they depend heavily on preserving their low wage advantages; and most start with larger internal imbalances (higher debt/GDP ratios, etc.). Some economists question whether the longer-run benefits from EMU will compensate for these costs without considerable Community support:

> Taken together there is strong macroeconomic and microeconomic evidence that the transition period to EMU will be anticohesive for the least advantaged regions. Although there will be longer-run gains, the transition has to be negotiated successfully first. It is highly unlikely that the possibility of longer-run gains for some will prove an adequate compensation for general short-run losses, both in achieving the transition to convergence and in implementing E-day. (Begg and Mayes 1992, p. 230)

There are thus grounds for questioning whether the recent doubling of the structural funds will adequately compensate the poorest regions for the costs of EMU. Begg and Mayes conclude that the Community will almost certainly have to contemplate an 'inter-regional equalisation system' if it is serious about cohesion. If so, the ECU 1 billion Cohesion Fund agreed at Maastricht was no more than a first limited step. A further doubling of the structural funds, if accompanied by improvements in targeting and administration, and a freeze (or preferably a gradual reduction) in real spending on agricultural price support, might just suffice, but it would probably be beyond the limits of political feasibility.

Conclusions

The overall impression from the foregoing review is that the economic case for moving to EMU is not conclusive, despite the Commission's research and responses to it. The economic issues are highly complex and the exercise unprecedented. A key difficulty is that the microeconomic effects of EMU are a marginal addition to a basic structural reform, the completion of the Single Market. Another is the huge uncertainty surrounding the impact of the change of monetary regime, particularly its contribution to price stability. A further complication is that circumstances differ considerably between EU economies.

According to the best empirical evidence, the direct, quantifiable benefits from EMU will be rather moderate. These are the static effects from savings in currency-conversion costs on intra-EC and, on a smaller scale, external transactions, from having a single currency. Possibly much more important, but harder to pin down, will be the benefits from removing intra-EC exchange-rate uncertainty. The long-run effect assuming a fairly full investment response to the lowering of the risk premium could be several percentage points added to GDP, although this is somewhat conjectural. This effect would be rather larger if the comparator situation were a more flexible exchange-rate regime (with the 15% band) implying larger pre-EMU risk premia, the removal of which would produce a larger investment stimulus. There would, however, be a downside risk to an EMU with an effective no-bailout rule but fiscal limits of questionable enforceability, in that real interest rates might then be raised in persistent high-deficit countries because of enhanced risk of government default, and there might be spillover effects from heavy government borrowing which could affect all participants. These risks will be discussed further in Chapter 8.

Large benefits are claimed for EMU's contribution to price stability, but they are open to debate. Difficult questions remain: are only formally independent banks operating totally outside political control capable of delivering price stability? If independence is necessary, is a central EC institution the best way of achieving it? And are the economic gains from price stability in terms of long-run activity and growth worth the costs incurred in achieving it, bearing in mind that independent central banks do not appear to have reduced the 'sacrifice ratio'? As yet, economic research does not have firm answers, and it may never solve them entirely. Such complex questions may always require 'political economy' judgments.

The other non-quantifiable benefits from EMU are either more speculative or probably modest in scale. Some economists believe that the gains from price transparency conferred by a single currency could be substantial in the long run, but the argument seems rather implausible. The Commission believe that there could in time be large gains from global policy cooperation when Europe has a single monetary policy, but their view has been strongly challenged. The other external benefits from international seigniorage and investor-portfolio reallocation under EMU seem unlikely to be major, although useful in the long run.

The potential costs from abandoning the exchange rate and national monetary policy as adjustment mechanisms are equally hard to assess. Although it may be true that core Member States have not been highly vulnerable to asymmetric shocks, important shocks of this nature have occurred at intervals and may happen again. The core States may be able to cope with them without serious mishap by virtue of their high industrial integration – but it cannot be ruled out that further integration will lead to more regional specialization. Large disturbances like the oil-price shocks and German reunification have proved difficult to manage. Moreover model-based simulations do not conclusively show that EMU would cope better with random shocks than floating would. The peripheral States are almost certainly less capable of managing asymmetric shocks, being less integrated, and the loss there of any freedom to pursue monetary policy directed to local stabilization could be important at times. They face an uncertain choice between retaining interest-rate flexibility to cope with asymmetric shocks and securing the lower general level of real interest rates that EMU may well offer.

Real-wage rigidities are a serious problem in most EC States at present, although not uniformly, and it would be optimistic to count on EMU breaking them down quickly. EMU might even add to them if greater wage transparency and labour mobility encourage a levelling up of real wages. In this respect, it is worrying that there are large sheltered wage sectors in some EC economies, mainly on the periphery. Prices in sheltered sectors are likely to continue to rise faster than average tradable prices after EMU. If so, and tradable sector wages in the affected economies are pulled up in the process, they will tend to become progressively less competitive and activity will suffer. Admittedly, greater competitive pressures under EMU and the Single Market may eventually lead to shrinkage of sheltered sectors, but it may take time and add to unemployment in the medium term.

Any relief to adjustment problems from removing national balance-of-payments constraints under EMU seems bound to be ephemeral. Persistent balance-of-payments deficits may be symptoms of domestic imbalance and there are serious risks in ignoring them.

Fiscal policy will probably be called upon to play a more active stabilization role under EMU, and there is evidence that national fiscal policy would be capable of coping with temporary shocks in most economies. However, national authorites will not be free to perform this function if there are rules in EMU restricting annual government deficits to small percentages of GDP, and they are rigidly enforced. There is no technical reason why fiscal stabilization could be not be provided alternatively and more efficiently through a central EC budget, and proposals of that kind have been made, but there seems little political support for them.

It seems out of the question that fiscal policy (i.e. stabilization) could cope with the structural problems which EMU will expose in weaker

EC economies. Other mechanisms are needed, and in most existing monetary unions the central budget makes an important contribution through *redistributive* taxes and transfer payments. The EU's redistributive mechanism is relatively limited, except in relation to the smallest and poorest countries. At present this is not an acute problem because the exchange rate is still available as an adjustment mechanism for non-core economies, as the upsets in the ERM since autumn 1992 have shown. However, it could become so under EMU if wage rigidities persist and productivity trends fail to converge. There is no guarantee that either will improve; some economists expect greater productivity divergence under EMU. The least developed regions may have most to gain from EMU in the very long run if they pursue appropriate policies, but EMU will intensify their adjustment task in the short and medium terms. This will no doubt add to pressures for greater Community support via the structural funds, but it seems questionable how much will be forthcoming, for political reasons. Private investment flows may play a greater transfer role in EMU, as they did under the gold standard, but they will only do so if the less developed economies manage to keep their costs under control and create an attractive investment environment.

In sum, it is no clearer from this research that the Community as a whole is an optimal monetary area, or even a 'feasible' one in Corden's sense. The core States probably comprise a feasible monetary union, although it may not be optimal if France is included. It seems highly questionable that all non-core States could safely join them to make a large, feasible, EMU in the near future. There are grounds for doubting whether the three or four smallest peripheral economies, and some of the larger ones, would be wise to join without more convergence or a considerable boost in EC financial support. Even for Britain as a comparatively large peripheral economy the economic calculus on its own is unclear, and leaves room for broader judgment.

It might be thought that if the economic evidence is so inconclusive, it does not matter; the question should be decided on other criteria – say foreign policy or security grounds. Economists sometimes seem to invite this response when they say that EMU has been motivated mainly by political objectives. However, such an inference would be a mistake: uncertainty about the economic consequences of EMU for some economies should not disguise the possibility that they could be hugely important, for better or worse. A better conclusion would be that the EMU question cannot be decided solely on technical argument; it entails judgments about priorities and risks which economists as technicians are not best placed to make. However, EMU is *par excellence* an economic issue. Accordingly the quality of 'political economy' judgments on it will be improved if they are informed by the best economic evidence, inconclusive though it is on its own. This thinking underlies the approach in the following chapters.

Chapter 7

The transition

This chapter reviews the process of transition to EMU, Stage II, with particular reference to the convergence criteria: their rationale, the prospects for Member States meeting them, and hence the timing of the move to Stage III. Consideration is also given to the roles of the EMI and the basket ECU in Stage II.

The rationale of transition

In the debates before the Treaty, almost as much attention was devoted to the process of reaching EMU as to EMU itself. Many of the most vexed issues arose in the former area, where several schools of thought were in contention. The 'monetarist' school held that full EMU ought to be introduced rapidly and with minimal conditions, in the belief that EC economies are sufficiently similar in structure and adaptable in market behaviour to allow almost any of them to join, even those with high inflation (Giovannini 1990). A more cautious school held that differences between some, perhaps most, EC economies are too great to permit painless adjustment to EMU after the event: an early move risked generating tensions that could damage the whole venture. On this view, EMU should not be formed until economies have securely converged. Some adherents emphasized convergence of inflation and related 'nominal' magnitudes, and others (the 'economist' school) emphasized 'real' or supply-side factors such as cost *levels* and labour-market flexibility. The cautious school came to the view that all States should have to pass certain explicit tests of performance before being admitted to EMU; whereas 'monetarists' felt such tests were mostly unnecessary if not damaging. A few 'economists' held that adequate convergence had already been established among a handful of States, including Germany and France, and urged them to form a small monetary union immediately (Dornbusch 1990).

A totally different body of opinion believed that transition should be a gradual market-based process, not driven by political decisions; this came to be characterized as the 'evolutionary' approach. One version, embraced by the British government, proposed the introduction a*s early as the start of Stage II* of a new currency, the 'hard ECU', which would be issued and managed by a new central monetary institution not unlike the ECB, and circulate alongside national currencies (Grice 1990). The hard ECU's function would be to reinforce convergence by providing an attractive alternative currency as strong as the strongest existing currency (effectively, the D-mark). The scheme was rejected for various reasons, some conflicting. Some opponents doubted the ability of the proposed European Monetary Fund to create a currency which would seriously rival the D-mark; others questioned the need for a new currency, if it was merely to supplement the D-mark; some believed that its gradual intro-duction would set back the achievement of EMU indefinitely; others believed that, far from being a gradual approach, the hard ECU's disci-pline would be too demanding.[1] However, the fact that it was put forward by a government which made no secret of its distaste for politically driven EMU was probably enough to kill the scheme.

In the event the 'nominal' convergence approach, being close to the views of core ERM governments, particularly Germany's, prevailed in the IGC. Their view was that all participants in EMU should be capable of taking the 'medicine' of a monetary policy modelled on German lines, and the criteria should test this. As Germany was the country with most to lose, this did not seem an unreasonable requirement to other IGC participants.

The convergence criteria

Inflation

The logic of the inflation criterion is straightforward: convergence of domestic inflation is a necessary precondition for successful EMU, on reasoning of a kind discussed in the preceding chapters. Convergence is to be assessed in terms of the annual rate of increase of a country's con-sumer price index relative to that of the 'three best-performing States' in the year before the examination, the permitted excess being 1½% (Treaty, 'Protocol on the convergence criteria', Article 1).[2] Although the Treaty refers to 'the achievement of a high degree of price stability', the criterion leaves the possibility that inflation may not be subdued prior to

Stage III. This would certainly add to the ECB's burden, and there have been suggestions that a maximum inflation rate should also be specified, but they have not attracted much support, such is confidence in the ability of the core States to control inflation.

Fiscal position

The *fiscal* criterion requires that participating governments should be in a sustainable financial position before EMU starts, again on reasoning of a kind discussed in the preceding chapters. Sustainability is to be assessed in terms of both the budget deficit (net borrowing of 'general government', i.e. central and regional or local government and social security funds), which should not exceed 3% of GDP at market prices; and the gross debt of general government (at nominal or 'book' values), which should not exceed 60% of GDP at market prices ('Protocol on the excessive deficit procedure', Articles 1 and 2).

The reference values for deficits and debts broadly reflect averages in the core of the Community in the years before the signing of the Treaty, since when most Member States' fiscal positions have deteriorated markedly, as will be seen. They also have a certain arithmetic logic, in that an economy with nominal GDP regularly rising at 5% p.a. (for example, 3% real growth and 2% inflation), an initial government debt/GDP ratio of 60% and annual net government borrowing of 3% of GDP will have a stable debt ratio. But although plausible, they have no unique validity; other combinations of nominal growth, deficits and debt ratios might be quite stable. Higher nominal growth and debt/GDP ratios are evidently sustainable in EC economies, as Belgium's case shows. In particular, it is not clear for all States that significantly higher debt ratios would be inconsistent with price stability.

It was recognized that judgment would be needed in the application of the fiscal criterion. The Treaty provides considerable latitude in relation to the debt ratio, but less in relation to the deficit ratio, as will be explained in Chapter 8. Ever since its announcement economists have worried that, without more flexibility, the 3% deficit ratio would create problems in Stage II. In the event it will prove hard for a number of Member States (around half) to approach the fiscal criterion in the foreseeable future despite strong retrenchment, and this has led to calls for its modification, as will be seen in the next chapter.

Exchange-rate stability

The *exchange-rate* criterion requires that countries demonstrate their fitness for EMU by maintaining a stable exchange rate within the ERM for an extended period before joining. This was accepted without much controversy in the EMU IGC, although some economists have doubted that membership of a narrow-band ERM says much about an economy's ability to survive in EMU (Kenen 1995a, Chapter 7). Even initially, the criterion was hard to interpret because its reference to the ERM was somewhat ambiguous, and the mechanism's radical relaxation in August 1993 has intensified the confusion.

There is little doubt that when those drafting the Treaty referred to 'the observance of the normal fluctuation margins' of the ERM for at least two years previously, 'without severe tensions' (*Treaty*, Article 109j.1 and 'Protocol on the convergence criteria', Article 3) they meant formal membership of the narrow band, which the Delors Committee had regarded as an essential precondition for EMU (Committee for the Study of Economic and Monetary Union 1989, p. 39). But as the narrow band has not been reinstated it cannot now feature in the criterion, although a number of States still view stability *within* the ERM as an important requirement. After the ERM upsets in 1993, the Commission came to accept that it is *de facto* stability which matters, although they have not been very precise as to what this means; their message seems to be that currencies must be within the 15% band, and must not have experienced 'large' fluctuations within it (Ravasio 1994, p. 9). However, that was before the further outbreak of currency turbulence in 1995 and this additional manifestation of the system's fragility might induce them, and conceivably in due course the Council, to take an even more relaxed view of stability in the transition to EMU.

Although the authorities in core States might well resist such a re-interpretation, most economists would support it. Since the ERM crises of 1992–3, scepticism has become widespread about the feasibility of adjustable-peg systems under conditions of high international capital mobility, as established after the complete removal of EC exchange controls. Economists of differing persuasions now mostly agree that living within the new wide band is probably the best approach for Stage II (Portes 1993; Williamson 1993b, De Grauwe 1994; Kenen 1995a, Chapter 7, among others), although they draw different conclusions. Some want to accelerate towards EMU; others, to pursue determined convergence policies under more flexible currency arrangements (more frequent realignments, less rigid bands); others to reintroduce exchange controls, or at least impose penalties on currency speculation that would put 'grit' in the system (Eichengreen and Wyplosz 1993). While rejecting the latter suggestion, Artis (1994) thought that a return to narrow bands, perhaps with 'soft edges' temporarily, might be feasible in Stage II if the Bundesbank could be persuaded to adopt a more 'European' monetary policy under EMI tutelage, but this was before the recent turbulence. Attention has turned to possible measures of exchange-rate stability outside the ERM framework. Proposals have been made for *average* measures which would allow marked but temporary deviations from a notional narrow band – for example observance of a *standard deviation* within 2¼% of the mean against the strongest currency, measured over periods of one or two years (Johnson 1994). Similar measures implying more or less stability could readily be calculated.

Whatever view is taken on these questions, it would be preferable to have clarification so that all concerned know what eligibility for Stage III entails; at the very least, it should be made clear whether two years' formal membership of the ERM is still required. Reinterpretation would not necessarily mean Treaty amendment: Article 6 of the 'Protocol on the convergence criteria' gives the Council the power to lay down their details. Admittedly the scope for relaxation will be limited in practice, for unanimity would be required, and any interpretation will have to satisfy influential authorities who strongly oppose dilution of the convergence tests. They include not least the German government and Bundestag, whose determination to resist any weakening will have been boosted by the decision of the German Constitutional Court in October 1993, which required the government there to insist on a 'strict' interpretation of the convergence criteria. Unfortunately, if unsurprisingly in the circumstances, the ECOFIN Council seems loth to offer any clarification of this question pending the first assessments at end-1996.

Without such clarification, it will not be finally clear whether the near collapse of the ERM and subsequent bouts of currency pressure have hindered or helped the EMU process. Opponents of EMU greeted the currency turmoil of 1992–3 as corroboration of their view that Member States are insufficiently converged to warrant locking their exchange rates together, and the renewed turbulence of spring 1995 is held to add further corroboration. In contrast, EMU supporters believed that the realignments of 1992–3 helped to clear the way for an early move to Stage III, as the new pattern of parities is more sustainable and removes any need for 'one last realignment', which some had thought desirable. But while it now seems widely accepted by politicians as well as economists that it would be a mistake to return to the narrow-band ERM as an entry route to EMU, this has not been officially confirmed by governments. So long as the Council refrains from such recognition, the possibility that severe currency speculation will recur, and greatly complicate the final transition to Stage III, will not be totally removed.

Long-term interest rates

The logic of the *interest-rate* criterion is less clear-cut than that of the other criteria. The requirement that a Member State's long-term interest rate must not exceed the average of the three best-performing States (in terms of price stability) by more than two percentage points in the year preceding the examination is described as a test of 'the durability of convergence' (Article 109j.1). Convergence of long-term interest rates may reasonably be regarded as a forward-looking indicator of inflation convergence among EC economies in the longer term, in that long-term nominal-interest-rate differentials between currencies that are not subject to exchange controls are approximate indicators of relative inflation expectations. In addition, since long-term interest rates in most Member States are dominated by conditions in government bond markets, interest-rate convergence on the best performers may be taken to indicate market confidence in the sustainability of a government's financial position. Thus the interest-rate criterion may be interpreted as a supplementary test of both inflation and fiscal convergence.

This criterion has attracted two related criticisms. Some commentators have argued that a margin of 2% is too lax a test, in that long-term interest differentials among the ERM currencies have often differed by less, even where current and expected inflation were quite wide apart (Bishop 1991c). Long-term interest rates tended to be compressed within the ERM so long as the markets believed that its disciplines would ultimately work to narrow inflation differentials (if not necessarily in the short run). But those judgments were vulnerable, as the events of 1992–3 showed. More fundamentally, such critics have argued that long-term interest differentials cannot be a reliable indicator of convergence before EMU; small differentials may merely indicate that the market believes the relevant currencies will join EMU in the short/medium term, and do not necessarily reflect suitability to join. Thus the interest-rate criterion gives too rosy a picture.[3]

This view seems unduly sceptical. While interest differentials below 2% do not confirm that convergence is durable, they do provide a useful test. At least, larger differentials would be a worrying signal that either inflation or fiscal positions, or both, are not expected to converge closely in the longer term.

Real criteria

Compared with its emphasis on nominal convergence, the Treaty pays only minor attention to *real* convergence, although it is not totally ignored. The reports by the Commission and the EMI must also take account of 'the results of the integration of markets, the situation and development of the balances of payments on current account and an examination of the development of unit labour costs and other price indices' (*Treaty*, Article 109j.1, last paragraph); but no tests are specified and the weight to be given to them is unclear. Bearing in mind the emphasis on supply-side factors in the theory of optimal currency areas, and the concerns about real convergence in 'One Market, One Money' and elsewhere, the Treaty's sidelining of such factors is disturbing. There were of course reasons: most governments in the IGC were preoccupied with the monetary objectives of EMU, and those with structural problems were reluctant to highlight them. Furthermore, it is more difficult to measure real factors such as competitiveness and market flexibility than nominal magnitudes such as inflation and fiscal deficits – although the latter's interpretation may be controversial.

However, these difficulties should not detract from the crucial importance of 'real' factors to EMU. Inflation convergence was regarded as an essential precondition for Stage III because it was feared that price and cost divergence would create serious tensions after the event. But similar concerns apply equally, if not more, if there are large differences in price or cost *levels* at the start of Stage III.[4] Mere convergence of inflation would not be enough to reduce them: *disinflation* would be required in high-cost economies, and this would be a painful process.[5] Differences in price or cost levels would thus pose more difficult adjustment problems in Stage III than equivalent differences in inflation.

The absence of emphasis on price and cost relativities in the Treaty has been defended on the ground that competition will be promoted by the Single Market programme, so competitiveness need not feature in the EMU criteria. However, this optimism did not extend to inflation relativities, and it is illogical to be concerned about them but not relative levels. Another defence appealed to survey evidence from Eurostat and OECD sources that there were not major discrepancies in levels of EC tradable goods prices. But the evidence at the time was rather out of date, failing to take account of sharp movements since the mid-1980s. Also it is subject to two important qualifications. First, there are big differences in *non-tradables* prices, in sectors sheltered from international competition, and they will matter in EMU because non-tradables have a high weight in the cost of living, and are therefore important influences in wage determination. Secondly, partly for this reason and partly because labour markets tend to be less exposed to international pressures than goods markets, international *labour-cost* differences tend to be significantly larger than price differences, especially in the tradable sector. These price/cost discrepancies can imply large profitability differences, which have strong effects on investment and employment in the longer run, even though firms accept them in the short run.

Although it is widely accepted that there are problems in measuring international competitiveness, they are not insurmountable (see Turner and Van't dack 1993). Cost measures are less subject to these drawbacks than price measures, because they capture long-run influences like profit margins. Moreover it is not clear that levels estimates are substantially less reliable than corresponding rates of change. So while exclusion of competitiveness from the main Treaty criteria can be defended up to a point, the arguments are not decisive. Competitiveness measures certainly require careful interpretation, but so do the other criteria. Their omission risks leaving a major gap in the assessment of eligibility for Stage III.

The sidelining of the other 'real' factors mentioned in the Treaty (such as labour-market flexibility) is perhaps more defensible, given the severe problems of measurement and interpretation they suffer from. Nevertheless there are good reasons to take them into account. Asset prices, especially house prices, are important leading influences on inflation, not least via their role in wage determination. The external current account, purged of cyclical influences, is important because it measures the balance of supply and demand for domestic savings, and thus a State's likely call on the union's savings. The unemployment rate, if interpreted with care, can be a useful indicator of labour-market flexibility, especially if supplemented by measures of its duration and variability, and of vacancies. The convergence reports should give full attention to all these indicators.

Prospects for convergence

Inflation

As may be seen from Table 7.1, EC inflation has fallen substantially and converged markedly since the mid-1980s. Low commodity-price inflation has helped, but there have been important contributions from lower wage increases, in part due to the recession, and higher productivity growth. In the past four years, the rise in the price deflator for private consumption in the three best-performing States has averaged about 2% p.a., tending

Table 7.1: Price deflator of private consumption, EU-15 States (% change on previous year) (annual averages)

Country	1974–85	1986–90	1991–4	1995	1996
Belgium	7.5	2.3	**2.4**	1.9	**2.4**
Denmark	9.6	3.7	**1.7**	2.3	2.7
Germany			3.8	2.3	2.5
W. Germany	4.6	1.5	3.4	2.0	2.4
Greece	17.5	17.1	14.6	9.6	8.9
Spain	15.4	6.6	5.9	4.9	4.5
France	10.5	2.9	**2.4**	**1.9**	**2.1**
Ireland	13.7	2.9	2.5	2.9	2.7
Italy	16.0	5.9	5.5	5.2	4.5
Luxembourg	7.4	2.6	2.9	2.3	2.5
Netherlands	5.7	0.9	2.6	**1.8**	**2.2**
Portugal	22.2	11.7	8.9	4.5	4.5
UK	12.0	5.0	4.5	2.9	3.0
Austria	5.9	2.0	3.5	2.8	2.9
Finland	10.8	4.5	3.8	**1.7**	3.3
Sweden	10.2	6.5	5.3	3.2	3.2
Europe[a]	10.8	4.2	4.4	3.2	3.2

[a] Aggregated with West Germany up to 1991; with Germany from 1992 onwards.
Note: Data in bold indicate the three best-performing States annually after 1991.
Source: European Commission. Data for 1994 onwards are Commission forecasts (May 1995).

to decline a little. Among the EC-12, Denmark and France have been consistently among the best performers, while Belgium, Ireland and the Netherlands have been close to the best. Inflation in Germany rose sharply in 1991–2, reflecting reunification and associated increases in indirect taxes, but has since come down. In 1994 the three best performers were France, Denmark and the Netherlands, while five States (Belgium, Germany, Ireland, Luxembourg and the UK) were within 1½% of their average.

According to Commission forecasts completed in May 1995 (Commission 1995a), inflation in the best-performing States is set to be just over 2% in the next two years, rising slightly. These forecasts must be treated with more than usual caution, because they do not take account of exchange-rate developments after March 1995.[6] The emergence of moderately-paced recovery in most EC economies (see Table 7.2), due to monetary-policy relaxation in Germany and elsewhere, is expected to

Table 7.2: GDP at constant prices, EU-15 States (% change on preceding year) (annual averages)

Country	1974–85	1986–90	1991–4	1995	1996
Belgium	1.8	3.0	1.2	2.7	2.6
Denmark	2.0	1.4	2.0	3.3	2.9
Germany			2.3	3.0	2.6
W. Germany	1.7	3.4	1.9	2.5	2.2
Greece	2.5	1.7	1.2	1.6	1.8
Spain	1.9	4.5	1.0	3.1	3.4
France	2.2	3.2	0.8	3.1	2.9
Ireland	3.8	5.1	4.6	6.9	5.5
Italy	2.8	3.0	0.9	3.3	3.4
Luxembourg	1.8	4.6	2.5	3.3	2.9
Netherlands	1.8	3.1	1.6	3.2	2.8
Portugal	2.2	5.1	0.8	3.0	3.2
UK	1.4	3.3	0.8	3.1	2.8
Austria	2.2	3.0	1.8	2.7	2.5
Finland	2.7	3.4	-2.1	5.3	4.2
Sweden	1.8	2.3	-0.7	2.8	3.0
Europe[a]	2.0	3.3	1.2	3.1	2.9

[a]Aggregated with West Germany up to 1991; with Germany from 1992 onwards.
Source: European Commission. Data for 1994 onwards are Commission forecasts (May 1995).

generate few inflationary pressures, and the sharp exchange deprecia-tions in March contribute only a limited boost to prices, except in Italy. The high-inflation States continue to converge on the core, albeit fairly gradually.

Fiscal position
EC government deficits have mostly risen sharply since the late 1980s, having previously fallen from the rather high levels of the early 1980s, thanks partly to the buoyant growth in the second half of the decade (Table 7.3). Recession has been a major factor in the fiscal deterioration of the early 1990s, working mainly through the automatic stabilizers, but also partly through discretionary action to cushion the downturn (Commission of the European Communities 1994). Assuming that the pickup in activity which emerged around 1994 continues, deficits will have mostly peaked around 1993. Thus only a few States currently meet the Treaty reference value for deficits, or can be confident of doing so

Table 7.3: General government lending (+) or borrowing (-), EU-15 States (% of GDP) (annual averages)

Country	1974–85	1986–90	1991–4	1995	1996
Belgium	-8.2	-7.0	-6.3	-4.2	-3.9
Denmark	-2.8	0.9	-3.4	-1.9	-1.2
Germany[a]			-3.0	-2.1	-2.4
W. Germany	-2.8	-1.5			
Greece		-13.0	-12.4	-11.3	-10.2
Spain	-2.8	-3.8	-5.8	-6.0	-4.8
France	-1.7	-1.8	-4.6	-4.9	-3.9
Ireland	-10.5	-5.5	-2.3	-2.8	-2.6
Italy	-9.6	-10.8	-9.6	-7.9	-8.1
Luxembourg	2.1	0.0	1.9	1.4	1.5
Netherlands	-3.9	-5.1	-3.3	-3.2	-2.5
Portugal		-5.0	-5.7	-5.6	-4.7
UK	-3.7	-1.1	-5.9	-4.8	-2.9
Austria	-2.4	-3.2	-3.1	-4.6	-3.9
Finland	3.7	4.0	-5.2	-5.0	-1.1
Sweden	-1.7	3.2	-8.2	-9.1	-5.8
Europe[b]	-4.1	-3.7	-5.3	-4.5	-3.9

[a] Not including unification-related debt assumptions by the federal government in 1995 (Treuhand and eastern housing companies) equal to DM236 bn.
[b] Aggregated with West Germany up to 1991; with Germany from 1992 onwards.
Source: European Commission. Data for 1994 onwards are Commission forecasts (May 1995).

soon. In the four years to 1994, only Ireland and Luxembourg have consistently had deficits lower than 3% of GDP. However, in 1994, unified Germany appears to have met the reference value, while the Netherlands came within one percentage point of it. Commission forecasts suggest that most deficits will fall gradually in 1995–6 on the strength of further fiscal retrenchment and economic recovery, but only seven States among the EC-15 (Denmark, Finland, Germany, Ireland, Luxembourg, Netherlands and the UK) are forecast to be below the 3% reference value by 1996, with a further three (Austria, Belgium and France) getting to within one percentage point of it. There are expected to be significant falls in Portugal and Spain, and particularly in the UK and Belgium, both of which are set to make large fiscal cuts; but progress is expected to stall somewhat in Italy.

Of the ten States among the EC-15 that are projected to be within or fairly close to the prescribed deficit ratio by 1996, three (Belgium,

**Table 7.4: General government gross debt, EU-15 States
(% of GDP)**

Country	1991	1994	1996
Belgium	130.1	136.1	132.3
Denmark	64.6	75.6	75.4
Germany	41.5	50.1	58.1
Greece	86.1	114.1	116.2
Spain	45.8	62.3	65.2
France	35.7	48.5	52.8
Ireland	96.9	89.8	80.8
Italy	101.3	125.4	124.4
Luxembourg	4.9	7.2	7.8
Netherlands	78.9	78.1	77.1
Portugal	69.3	69.2	70.7
UK	35.7	50.1	51.5
Austria	58.7	64.5	67.4
Finland	23.0	60.1	64.6
Sweden	53.0	79.1	85.7
Europe[a]	56.0	68.1	70.4

[a] Aggregated with West Germany up to 1991; with Germany from 1992 onwards.
Source: European Commission. Data for 1994 onwards are Commission forecasts (May 1995).

Ireland and the Netherlands) will still have high debt ratios (Table 7.4); and even Germany's debt ratio is not far below 60% then. Belgium is forecast still to have a debt ratio well over twice the reference value and not falling much, as well as a marginally high deficit, in contrast to its good inflation performance. Among the new members, only Finland is forecast to meet the reference value for the fiscal deficit by 1996; Austria exceeds it moderately, although converging, but Sweden by a wide margin. Reflecting their large deficits in recent years, all three are projected to exceed the critical debt ratio, but Austria and Finland only marginally. Sweden, however, is expected to have serious debt and deficit problems for some time.

The Commission's fiscal forecasts, which are based on known policy actions, are less optimistic than Member States' projections in their official convergence programmes, and so far the outturns tend to bear the Commission out. The Community's general concern about fiscal developments is shown by the fact that 10 of the EC-12 States were found by

Figure 7.1: Deviations from the D-mark within the ERM (old narrow-band currencies) [a]

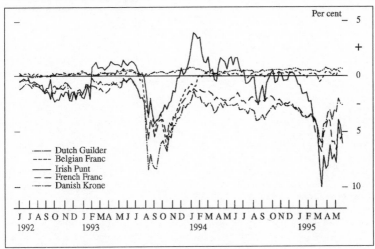

Source: Bank of England.

[a] Deviations from the ERM central rate compared to the D-mark deviation from the same rate.

Figure 7.2: Deviations from the D-mark within the ERM (other current ERM currencies) [a]

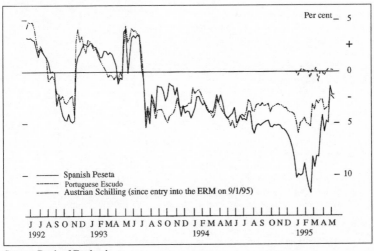

Source: Bank of England.

[a] Deviations from the ERM central rate compared to the D-mark deviation from the same rate.

Figure 7.3: Deviations from the D-mark outside the ERM (sterling,[a] Italian lira,[a] Swedish krona[b] and Finnish markka[b])

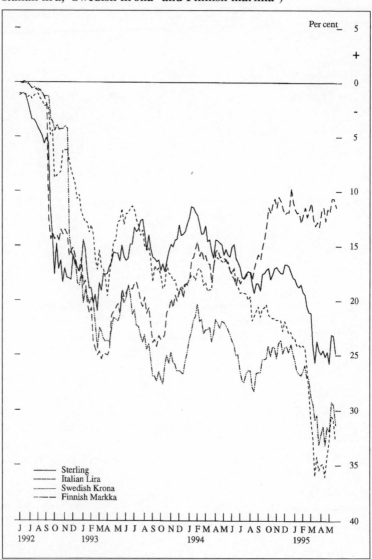

Legend:
— Sterling
--- Italian Lira
------ Swedish Krona
--- Finnish Markka

Source: Bank of England.

[a] After exit from system, deviations are from last ERM central rate against the D-mark.

[b] Deviations are from market rate against the D-mark on 5 June 1992.

ECOFIN to have excessive deficits when the formal procedure was first adjudicated in September 1994. Ireland, however, was not among them, suggesting that there can be more latitude in the assessment of debt ratios (where Ireland is 'high', but 'sufficiently diminishing') than of deficit ratios (where it is 'low').

Exchange rates

Most of the currencies which remained in the ERM through the turmoil of 1992–3, and which had previously been in the narrow band, had returned within or fairly close to the *notional* narrow band by about March 1994 (Figure 7.1). Survival was not without periodic stress in some cases, as illustrated by the raising of Danish short-term interest rates to emergency levels in the winter of 1992–3 and again in the summer and autumn of 1993, when Belgian rates also had to be raised sharply; but short-term interest differentials against German rates subsequently fell back (Figure 7.4 below). The Irish pound was devalued by 10% in February and depreciated further in the summer, but recovered quite strongly later in the year, along with sterling. Of the other currencies that devalued or left the mechanism, the peseta and escudo stabilized at lower levels against the D-mark for about a year following the mid-1993 crisis (Figure 7.2) – at around 12% and 22% respectively below their mid-1992 levels. The lira had also depreciated against the D-mark by about 20% from its earlier level by March 1993, having left the mechanism in September 1992 (Figure 7.3). It subsequently rallied until the August crisis, after which it depreciated continuously if unevenly against the D-mark. Sterling, having left the ERM with the lira, initially depreciated by about 18% against the DM, but regained around a third of that depreciation by mid-1993 and thereafter broadly held its ground for nearly a year.

Among the new members, the Finnish markka and the Swedish krona, having been compelled to sever their link with the ECU in the crisis of September 1992 despite sharp hikes in short-term interest rates, had both depreciated by some 25% against the D-mark by the start of 1993 (Figure 7.3). Following this adjustment, their short-term interest-rate differentials against the D-mark could be reduced to around 1% and they recovered somewhat to mid-1993. After the August crisis the markka tended to strengthen quite strongly, if unevenly, against the D-mark, while the Swedish krona moved erratically, barely holding its own with the mark. In contrast, the markets never doubted the will and ability of the Austrian authorities to maintain the long-established link between the schilling and the D-mark, and it remained little affected through the upsets of 1992–3.

Renewed exchange-market turbulence broke out in the early months of 1995, reflecting a new collapse of confidence in the US dollar and a flight to the D-mark as a 'safe-haven' currency. This created new tensions within the ERM, with the more suspect European currencies all suffering strong downward pressure, to varying extents, whereas only the guilder and schilling, joined this time by the Belgian franc, remained firm against the D-mark. Increases in interest rates on the currencies under pressure (Figures 7.4 and 7.5), combined with a relaxation of German monetary policy and concerted central-bank intervention in support of the dollar, have permitted them to recover somewhat, and none of the ERM currencies breached the 15% band. But by summer 1995 only the guilder, schilling and Belgian franc were securely within the *notional* narrow band against the D-mark, and the French franc among others was still well below it.

The start of the two-year reference period for the first assessment of exchange-rate performance under the convergence criterion must date from no later than January 1995, given that the examination is to be by the end of 1996. Forecasts of exchange rates are inherently hazardous, as the renewed turbulence in 1995 illustrates. To be sure of meeting the criterion, currencies of EC-12 States must have been formally within the ERM by January 1995, and if it is interpreted strictly they must presumably remain within or fairly close to the *notional* narrow band from then on. Alternatively, if the Council chose to interpret the criterion in a more relaxed way, observance of the 15% band 'without severe tensions' might suffice. If formal membership of the ERM nevertheless remains a requirement, the lira and sterling clearly would not now meet it, having been suspended from the system, while the devaluations of the peseta and the escudo in March 1995 presumably also disqualify them. The three new Member States are not required to be formal members of the ERM (although Austria has joined), but their currencies will need to show a degree of stability similar to the core ERM currencies in the period to end-1996 if they are to meet the test then.

Interest rates
In the six months or so following the ERM relaxation in August 1993, EC long-term interest rates largely predicted a resumption of the inflation convergence seen previously, with one or two exceptions (Figures 7.6 and 7.7). In September 1993, the average rate on benchmark 10-year government bonds in the three States with the lowest inflation rates (Denmark, France and the Netherlands) was 6.3%, and corresponding

Figure 7.4: 3-month interest rates: deviations from the D-mark (old narrow-band ERM currencies and Austrian schilling)

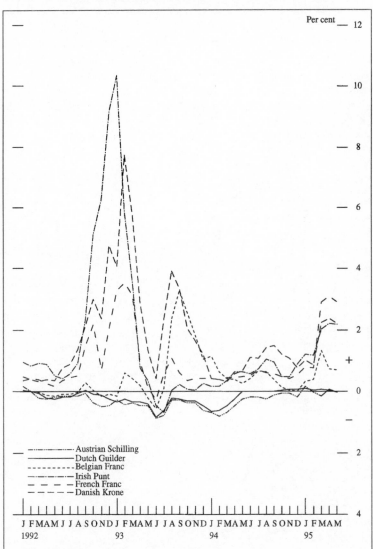

Source: Bank of England.

Figure 7.5: 3-month interest rates: deviations from the D-mark (other current ERM currencies, sterling and Italian lira)

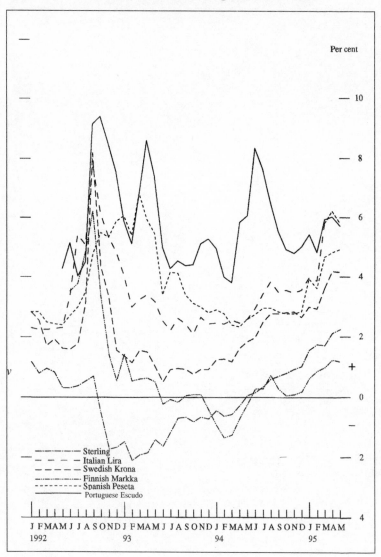

Source: Bank of England.

Figure 7.6: 10-year bond yields: deviations from the D-mark (old narrow-band ERM currencies and Austrian schilling)

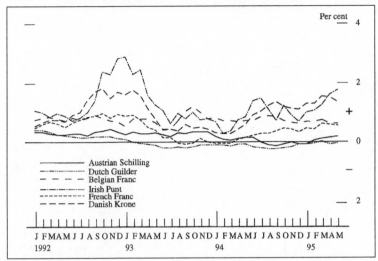

Source: Bank of England.

Figure 7.7: 10-year bond yields: deviations from the D-mark (other current ERM currencies, sterling and Italian lira)

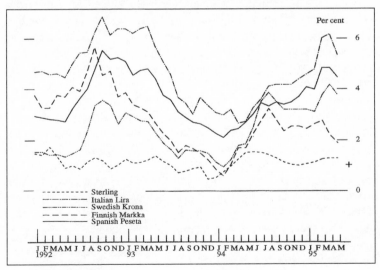

Source: Bank of England.

Table 7.5: Long-term interest rates (annual averages)

Country	1974–85	1986–90	1991–4	1995	1996
Belgium	10.6	8.5	**8.2**	8.2	**7.9**
Denmark	16.0	10.8	**9.4**	8.9	8.9
Germany			7.4	7.4	7.5
W. Germany	8.0	6.8			
Spain		12.9	11.1	11.9	11.3
France	12.2	9.1	**8.0**	**8.1**	**8.0**
Ireland	14.6	10.2	8.5	8.7	8.7
Italy	15.1	12.3	12.2	12.2	12.2
Netherlands	9.4	7.1	7.7	**7.8**	**7.9**
Portugal		17.1	14.3	10.9	10.5
UK	13.0	9.9	8.7	8.9	8.8
Austria	8.9	7.4	7.6	7.4	7.5
Finland	11.2	11.7	10.1	**9.4**	9.5
Sweden	11.0	11.7	10.0	10.4	10.0
Europe[a]	11.9	9.8	9.0	8.9	8.8

[a] Aggregated with West Germany up to 1991; with Germany from 1992 onwards.
Note: Data in bold indicate three States with lowest inflation annually after 1991.
Source: European Commission. Data for 1994 onwards are Commission forecasts (May 1995).

rates in three other States (Belgium, Germany and the UK) were within one percentage point. Luxembourg and Ireland had no precisely corresponding rates to report, but their rates on other maturities had been consistently within 1½% of the best inflation performers, while Austrian long-term rates barely deviate from German rates. However, the exchange-rate turbulence in early 1995 has led to some upward revisions in long-term interest differentials on the weaker currencies, reflecting heightened exchange risk and upward revision of inflation expectations. Rates in Italy, Portugal, Spain, Finland and Sweden have been particularly affected, and are forecast to be more than two percentage points adrift of the best performers by 1996 (Table 7.5), as are Greek rates (not shown). Finland's long-term rates may, however, move within the prescribed range if the better inflation and fiscal prospects there are consolidated. The UK's long-term rates have so far responded only moderately to sterling's recent weakness, suggesting that inflation expectations there remain subdued.

These forecasts, like those for inflation, depend heavily on the technical assumption of constant exchange rates after March 1995. Clearly

Table 7.6: Balance on external current account, EU-15 States (% of GDP) (annual averages)

Country	1974–85	1986–90	1991–4	1995	1996
Belgium	-1.5	1.6	3.4	5.8	5.7
Denmark	-3.5	-2.1	2.1	1.4	1.9
Germany			-1.4	-1.8	-1.8
W. Germany	0.8	4.2			
Greece	-2.5	-4.8	-3.9	-2.3	-2.6
Spain	-1.4	-1.3	-2.6	-1.9	-1.8
France	-0.3	-0.3	0.4	0.9	0.8
Ireland	-7.7	-1.2	4.7	6.9	6.8
Italy	-0.7	-0.6	-0.4	2.7	3.4
Luxembourg	27.1	33.6	28.5	26.1	24.7
Netherlands	1.9	3.0	3.7	4.7	4.9
Portugal	-5.8	-0.7	-1.7	-0.2	-0.4
UK	-0.1	-3.8	-1.9	-0.2	0.4
Austria	-1.0	0.1	-0.4	-1.4	-1.2
Finland	-2.0	-3.2	-2.5	2.4	1.4
Sweden	-1.7	-1.6	-1.8	0.7	2.0
Europe[a]	-0.3	0.1	-0.6	0.3	0.5

[a] Aggregated with West Germany up to 1991; with Germany from 1992 onwards.
Source: European Commission. Data for 1994 onwards are Commission forecasts (May 1995).

convergence of both inflation and interest rates could be at risk if the next few years see substantial further depreciation of the peripheral currencies against the core.

External balance and competitiveness

Having deteriorated during the period of buoyant growth in the second half of the 1980s, most States' *external current-account balances* have improved overall since around 1991, in part reflecting the recession (Table 7.6). However, the picture for the EC as a whole has been dominated by Germany, which experienced a pronounced shift into external deficit after reunification, partly reflecting its assumption of large deficits among the eastern *Länder*. France in contrast has been near external balance throughout, and is forecast to continue so. Belgium has consistently run current-account surpluses despite large fiscal deficits, and they seem set to continue. Denmark's earlier chronic payments deficit has

Figure 7.8: Unit labour costs in manufacturing – real effective exchange rates relative to EC-15 (1987 Q1 = 100)

(a) Low-inflation states

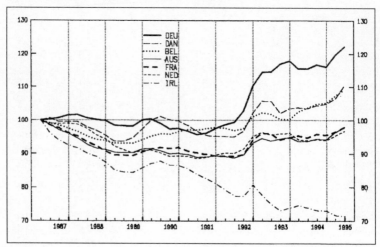

(b) Higher-inflation states

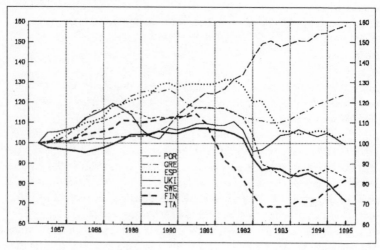

Source: Commission of the EC.

been transformed into comfortable surplus. Ireland, like Denmark, has moved from external deficit to large surplus. Italy's persistent deficit gave way to modest surplus after the lira left the ERM, and this is forecast to increase steeply. The UK's deficit started to improve earlier, when the economy moved towards deep recession in 1989, but the improvement stalled in the early 1990s until the effects of the depreciation of autumn 1992 started to come through, since when a marked further improvement to approximate balance has been established, despite the economic upswing.

Although these movements partly reflect changing cyclical positions, the substantial swings in *competitiveness* of the past few years must also be playing a part, albeit with the usual fairly long lags. Figure 7.8 shows the measure generally accepted as most relevant to trade performance – relative unit labour costs in manufacturing (in a common currency), expressed as index numbers of 'real effective exchange-rates' against the average for the EC-15. (A rise in the index represents a loss in competitiveness.) The low-inflation States at the core of the ERM mostly gained competitiveness in the period of exchange-rate stability between early 1987 and early 1992, whereas those with higher inflation, especially Portugal, Spain and Greece, tended to lose it. But these changes were mainly reversed between late 1991 and the end of 1993, when the core-ERM countries lost competitiveness sharply through currency appreciation, and those that devalued or left the system gained it. The picture since 1993 has been more diverse, but on the whole the weak-currency economies have maintained their better competitiveness or improved it further, whereas it has mostly deteriorated further among the strong-currency block. Particularly notable is the D-mark's large real appreciation (some 17% higher than in 1987), and the real depreciation of the lira (some 22% lower) and of the Irish pound. Sterling's real depreciation in 1992–3 more than reversed its earlier real appreciation, but some of this improvement was subsequently lost when sterling strengthened overall.

The persistent improvement in Ireland's external current account must owe something to its lower real exchange rate, and the Netherlands' strong external position may partially reflect the lagged effects of earlier competitiveness gains there. The more recent improvements in the Italian and UK payments positions must be partly attributable to their improved competitiveness; conversely, the substantial deterioration in Germany's external position must partly reflect the large loss of competitiveness there.

95

Table 7.7: Relative unit labour costs in manufacturing, selected industrial and developing countries[a] (Europe = 100)

Country	1990[b]	Oct. 1993[b]	Oct. 1995[c]
France	100.3	103.9	102.4
Germany	107.3	125.1	124.6
Italy	93.7	78.5	77.6
UK	101.5	92.3	92.6
Belgium	93.4	91.5	89.3
Netherlands	84.3	94.4	91.5
Sweden	102.4	77.5	79.8
Europe[d]	100.0	100.0	100.0
USA	69.9	73.1	
Japan	77.3	121.3	
South Korea	32.3	34.4	
Taiwan	54.9	59.4	

[a] Average hourly compensation in manufacturing industry divided by output per man hour, valued in a common currency at purchasing power parity exchange rates. Relative to average for 'Europe'.
[b] Estimates for 1990 (year) and Oct. 1993 from Turner and Van't dack (1993), Table 15, rebased to give 'Europe' = 100.
[c] Author's projections, derived from EC Commission forecasts of changes in whole economy unit labour costs, adjusted for relative trend productivity growth in manufacturing. Assumes no overall change in exchange rates, Oct. 1993– Oct. 1995.
[d] Weighted average of above seven countries, using PPP-valued GDP weight in 1990 (see Turner and Van't dack 1993).

It is nevertheless hard to judge from index numbers whether the real exchange rates seen since the ERM crisis are likely to be sustainable. Economists have proposed several alternative measures of sustainable rates. The traditional kind is based on purchasing power parities drawn from relative national-currency prices of a representative bundle of consumer goods and services (the PPP approach). A newer sort relies on the simulation of econometric models to derive a 'fundamental equilibrium exchange rate' – the FEER approach, developed by Williamson (see, for example, Williamson 1991). Neither is fully satisfactory and their results conflict somewhat.

A recent development of the PPP approach compares national *levels* of unit labour costs (Turner and Van't dack 1993). This is potentially superior to the traditional approach (because it captures differences in profit margins), although there are still significant measurement problems, especially in the valuation of national outputs. Table 7.7 offers estimates for seven European countries, together with a few others for comparison; all are measured in a common currency,[7] with the average for the European seven taken as 100. It appears that in 1990, the base year of the exercise, there were quite large cost differences between European economies, with Germany somewhat above the average and Italy and Benelux below. At that time both the other industrial majors were more competitive than 'Europe', with costs some 25–30% below the latter's; and newly industrializing Asian economies, represented by South Korea and Taiwan, were far more competitive – with costs as much as 40–70% below the European average. Europe's position against the United States had not changed much by late 1993, slightly faster US cost inflation having been more than offset by depreciation of the US dollar; and the European position against the Asian NICs had improved slightly too. Japan had, however, become much less competitive against all the others, owing to the yen's substantial nominal appreciation.

Meanwhile large movements took place within Europe during the ERM upsets. In particular, the combination of an appreciating D-mark and (for Germany) unusually fast wage inflation led to the rapid emergence of high labour costs there. Relative costs in the Netherlands also rose somewhat, carried up by the guilder's link with the D-mark. In contrast relative costs in the depreciating countries – Sweden, Italy and the United Kingdom – fell markedly. Projections for the European countries to late 1995, based on a conventional assumption that there will be no overall change in their exchange rates, imply that the European cost relativities will not change much in the near future. In particular, Germany remains a very high-cost producer, with costs of the order of 35–40% above those of Benelux and 60% above Italy's. French costs remain near the European average, and UK costs rather below that average. The further currency movements during the first half of 1995 clearly cast doubt on this illustrative exchange-rate assumption; unless unwound, they are likely to widen yet further the cost discrepancies between the D-mark bloc and the peripheral economies.

Unemployment
Having fallen somewhat during the upswing of the late 1980s, *unemployment* started to rise again in most Member States around 1991, earlier in some (Denmark, the UK), later in others (Germany, the Netherlands),

Table 7.8: Unemployment,[a] EU-15 States (% of civilian labour force, annual averages)

Country	1974–85	1986–90	1991–4	1995	1996
Belgium	8.1	9.4	8.2	9.6	9.1
Denmark	6.4	6.7	9.8	8.6	8.0
Germany			7.1	7.8	7.3
W. Germany	4.2	5.9	5.3	6.3	6.0
Greece	4.0	7.4	8.9	9.6	9.5
Spain	11.2	18.9	20.5	23.7	22.8
France	6.4	9.8	11.0	12.1	11.5
Ireland	9.7	14.6	15.0	14.1	13.1
Italy	7.3	10.1	10.2	11.4	10.9
Luxembourg	1.7	2.1	2.5	3.6	3.4
Netherlands	7.3	7.8	6.4	7.6	7.2
Portugal	6.9	6.0	5.2	6.7	6.3
UK	6.9	8.9	9.7	8.3	7.8
Austria	2.5	3.4	3.8	3.9	3.8
Finland	4.8	4.4	14.3	16.3	14.6
Sweden	2.4	1.8	6.0	7.2	6.5
Europe[b]	6.5	9.1	9.9	10.7	10.1

[a] SOEC definition. OECD data for Austria, Finland and Sweden.
[b] Aggregated with West Germany up to 1991; with Germany from 1992 onwards.
Source: European Commission. Data for 1994 onwards are Commission forecasts (May 1995).

according to the timing of the economic downturn. With the emergence of recovery around 1994 (earlier in the UK), unemployment will have peaked then or slightly later. It is set to fall in most States, although only gradually in some, and the overall decline in the next two years is likely to be small (Table 7.8). Generally unemployment seems set to remain well above historical EC levels for the foreseeable future, and rather higher than in the previous trough of activity in the early/middle 1980s. This suggests some further deterioration in the Community's underlying unemployment situation due to structural factors, including persistently poor external competitiveness, as is now officially recognized, for example in the Commission's 1994 White Paper.

It is not easy to assess how far the Community is from sustainable levels of unemployment and which economies are particularly affected. A rough impression may be obtained by comparing the annual average unemployment rate for the period 1991–6 (including Commission fore-

Table 7.9: Structural unemployment estimates, EU-15 States[a]
(% of civilian labour force) (annual averages)

Country	[a] 1974–85	[b] 1991–6[b]	[c] Increase (b)-(a)
High (>4%)			
Spain	11.2	21.4	10.2
Finland	4.8	14.7	9.9
Greece	4.0	9.1	5.1
France	6.4	11.3	4.9
Ireland	9.7	14.5	4.8
Medium (2-4%)			
Sweden	2.4	6.3	3.9
Italy	7.3	10.5	3.2
Denmark	6.4	9.3	2.9
U.K.	6.9	9.1	2.2
Low (<2%)			
W. Germany	4.2	5.6	1.4
Austria	2.5	3.8	1.3
Luxembourg	1.7	2.8	1.1
Belgium	8.1	8.6	0.5
Netherlands	7.3	6.7	-0.6
Portugal	6.9	5.6	-1.3

[a] The increase in structural unemployment is estimated as the difference between columns (a) and (b).
[b] Includes Commission forecasts for 1994, 1995 and 1996.

casts), which includes three years of recession and three of recovery, with the average for the 12 years 1974–85, representing conditions in the Community after the first oil-price shock but before the major deterioration in external competitiveness. Table 7.9 divides the 15 economies into groups with 'high', 'medium' and 'low' increases in structural unemployment. On this measure, all Member States except Portugal and the Netherlands have experienced some rise.[8] In some (Finland, Spain, Ireland, Greece and France) it has been considerable – more than four percentage points; Sweden and Italy too have experienced sizeable increases (over three percentage points). Thus although structural labour-market problems are spread fairly widely across the Community, they look to be most acute in these seven economies.

Table 7.10: Likely eligibility for Stage III, EU-15 States, end-1996

Country	Inflation	Fiscal position	Exchange rate	Interest rate	Eligibility
Belgium	✓	✗	✓	✓	✗
Denmark	✓	✓	✓	✓	✓
Germany	✓	✓	✓	✓	✓
Greece	✗	✗	✗	✗	✗
Spain	✗	✗	✗	✗	✗
France	✓	(✗)	✓	✓	(✗)
Ireland	✓	✓	✓	✓	✓
Italy	✗	✗	✗	✗	✗
Luxembourg	✓	✓	✓	✓	✓
Netherlands	✓	✓	✓	✓	✓
Portugal	✗	✗	✗	✗	✗
UK	✓	✓	✗	✓	✗
Austria	✓	(✗)	✓	✓	(✗)
Finland	✓	(✓)	✓	(✓)	(✓)
Sweden	✓	✗	✗	✗	✗

Notes
✓: meets Maastricht criterion.
✗: fails Maastricht criterion.
( ): result specially uncertain.
Source: Author's estimates (see text).

Meeting the criteria

Using the above forecasts, a provisional assessment can be made of which States will meet the convergence criteria in the first examination by end-1996. It must be tentative, since the forecasts are unusually uncertain, as explained, and no allowance is made for future policy changes. Moreover it is unclear how ECOFIN will interpret the criteria, and how much weight will be put on 'real' factors.

Best guesses for the EU-15 are summarized in Table 7.10, where brackets indicate that a guess is particularly uncertain. It seems likely on present policies that 11 States will meet the *inflation* criterion and 4 (Greece, Italy, Portugal and Spain), will not; 7 of those 11 will meet the fiscal criterion and 8 will not (Austria, Belgium, France, Greece, Italy, Portugal, Spain and Sweden); 9 will meet the exchange-rate criterion and 6 (Greece, Italy, Portugal, Spain, Sweden and the UK) will not;[9] and 10 will meet the interest-rate criterion while 5 (Greece, Italy, Portugal, Spain and Sweden) will not. Assuming that eligibility would require meeting all four criteria, even though the Treaty does not state this, it therefore appears that 6 States, a minority of the 15, would have a good chance of being found eligible on this reckoning.

However, Denmark has decided that it will not participate in EMU (but this could change after the next IGC) and if this exemption is maintained, 5 of 15 States would be counted as eligible – clearly a minority.[10] In that case EMU could not go ahead in 1997, as finance ministers presumably appreciated in reaching their provisional conclusion in June 1995. The outcome could depend on a number of individual performances and Council judgments. Belgium might mount an even stronger fiscal retrenchment which, with lower debt interest, could bring enough of a decline in its debt ratio to allow the Council to give it the benefit of the doubt, given its good inflation and ERM record. Conversely, there must be a serious risk that the improvements in the French and Finnish deficits will be less than projected, and there must be doubts about Finland's much improved perfomance generally.

More fundamentally, much could turn on future events in the foreign-exchange markets, and on the Council's interpretation of the exchange-rate criterion. If there is a re-emergence of downward pressure on the weaker EC currencies, or if the Council feels obliged to take a relatively strict view of the criterion (for example, with reference to the 'normal' band requirement), several more currencies might be found wanting, including perhaps the French franc, making an early EMU clearly out of reach.

In these circumstances, it is hardly surprising that finance ministers should now be inclined to rule out an early start to EMU. Even if, against expectations, ECOFIN were to find an eligible majority in the end-1996 assessments to be made under Treaty provisions, the Council (at the level of heads of State or government) would still have to decide (by qualified majority, including States with derogations and exemptions) whether it would be 'appropriate for the Community to enter the third stage'. There are enough unfavourable considerations in the economic sphere to suggest a negative view on wider grounds – worries about external competitiveness of the proposed union, the overall imbalance between monetary and fiscal policies, the questionable sustainability of inflation performance in the light of the general cyclical situation, and high structural unemployment in the Community generally. In the political sphere a decision to move quickly to EMU without EC founder members like Italy and Belgium and major economies like Spain would risk serious damage to the EU's cohesion, whereas postponement for two years or so would not be disastrous politically, and it would give time for fiscal performances to improve, and for more progress on reducing unemployment, assuming the recovery proves more than usually robust.

A detailed forecast now of the economic position at end-1997, when the second examination is likely, is inevitably more hazardous.[11] The possibility cannot be ruled out that new developments, at present hard to foresee, could upset the Community's environment three or more years ahead. Further outbreaks of currency turbulence could make it difficult to establish the stability deemed necessary to allow the smooth locking of exchange rates by end-1998; and a widespread cyclical downturn later in the decade could recreate the fiscal problems which make an early EMU seem problematic, given the Treaty's emphasis on fiscal rectitude. However, the existing degree of slack in the EU economies and the gradualness of the present recovery suggest that an early downturn is unlikely, and with inflation pressures remaining subdued in Germany and the other core States, there is scope for further relaxation of monetary policy there, which should help relieve global currency tensions. Lower interest rates generally in the EU would help to reduce fiscal deficits. Assuming no new major exogenous shocks like reunification, the balance of probabilities thus still favours a continuation of economic convergence among EU States, and it is hard to see what other economic developments could drive the core economies so far off course that few or none could qualify for Stage III in 1999. One or two of the economies which now seem likely to be marginally ready then may encounter local shocks that would disqualify them temporarily, but others may by then have made further progress in overcoming their fiscal and inflation problems. Assuming, in addition, no important setbacks for EMU from the forthcoming political IGC and no major reverses of political direction in Germany or France (possibilities to be discussed later), a Stage III of six to seven States, or perhaps more, would seem clearly in prospect for 1999, when there will be no requirement for a majority – or for a judgment about 'appropriateness'.

The EMI

The EMI was set up to manage the transition to EMU and the Treaty provides that it will do so in two main ways – by strengthening the coordination of monetary policies to promote price stability, and by making the technical preparations for the establishment of the ESCB. In the policy field its functions can be no more than advisory, 'without prejudice to the responsibility of the competent authorities for the conduct of monetary policy within the respective Member States' (*EMI Statute*, Article 3). Yet its Council may formulate opinions and recommendations on monetary and exchange-rate policy, and related measures introduced by Member States, and submit them to governments and the Ministers' Council; and it may publish them. It must be consulted by the Council and the monetary authorities of Member States on draft legislative provisions within its field of competence; and it should 'normally' be consulted by the national monetary authorities before they take policy decisions.

In essence these powers are not radically different from those of its predecessor, the EC Governors' Committee, although the rights to be consulted are strengthened and formalized. That Committee was sparing in their use, but the EMI may be less self-effacing in due course. It is likely to take seriously its responsibility for implementing the monetary aspects of the 'broad guidelines' for economic policy drawn up under Article 103 of the Treaty. This may include reviewing Member States' inflation objectives, paths for attaining them, and their consistency across States; consultation on the suitability and consistency of Member States' intermediate targets for attaining their monetary objectives; monitoring and reporting on progress in achieving convergence objectives so far as they lie in the monetary sphere, as it is required to do annually to the Council; and recommending monetary-policy adjustments where considered necessary in the light of these objectives. These may seem fairly standard surveillance tasks, but Stage II will have several new features: the explicit convergence framework established in the Treaty; the EMI's role (along with the Commission) in reporting on eligibility for Stage III; the strong legal protection from political pressure which the Treaty accords the EMI Council; and the high profile which the EMI will increasingly acquire as the embryo ECB of Stage III. The fact that most of the central banks which form the EMI are becoming increasingly independent will also lend weight to its advice (Viñals 1994).

It remains to be seen how far the EMI will go in making its policy advice public. Its Council is likely to be cautious at first, knowing that consultation is a two-way process and that untimely disclosure of a difference of view with a member central bank could destabilize currencies. But it will hardly be able to avoid its convergence assessments becoming public by the end of 1996 and if it were to develop serious concerns about the thrust of national monetary policies or the fiscal/monetary mix it might feel bound to make them public earlier.[12] The national authorities will not be obliged to follow its advice, even if published, but they are unlikely to disregard it, since they will know that the EMI will have a key input into the Council's judgments of eligibility.

Apart from the routine functions of running the EMS which it took over from the EMCF, the only significant operational activity that the EMI may engage in under its Statute is a limited one in managing member central banks' foreign-exchange reserves. In this respect the EMI would be operating only as an agent, not a principal; any foreign-exchange dealing would have to be within strict guidance from the relevant central bank, to avoid cutting across national monetary and exchange-rate policies. If dealing and investment operations material-ized, they would give the EMI useful hands-on market experience, but not amount to 'practising' exchange-rate policy, as some of Stage II's architects originally intended. It is not yet clear whether any central banks will use this facility; apparently none did so in the EMI's first year of operation (European Monetary Institute 1995, p. 67).

The second of the EMI's main tasks, making the technical prepara-tions for Stage III, will occupy much of its attention. Among subjects to be tackled will be the technical basis for formulating the single monetary policy, and the instruments and procedures to be used (to be discussed in the next chapter); the supporting monetary statistics, some harmoniza-tion of which will be required for the implementation of the single monetary policy; related tasks such as the promotion of efficient cross-border payments systems, which will be essential if EMU is to confer microeconomic benefits; and preparations for the single currency. Ini-tially the EMI has concentrated mainly on the central banking aspects of the latter task, such as banknote printing and distribution, but it would be advisable for it to turn its attention to wider aspects of conversion, on which so far the Commission have mainly made the running.

The EMI is required to report annually to the EC institutions on these matters, together with progress on convergence and on the compatibility of member central banks' legal status with Treaty requirements. Despite the expected postponement of Stage III's start, it must specify 'the regulatory, organisational and logistical framework necessary for the ESCB to perform its tasks in the third stage' by end-1996 at the latest (*EMI Statute*, Article 4.2). This is a tall order, given the complexity of the issues and the extent to which national interests are involved. Moreover, whenever the ECB begins operations, it will need more than a blueprint, as will be seen in Chapter 8. That may be difficult, for it will not be known until quite near the start of Stage III which States will participate.

Thus whenever the decision to move to Stage III is taken, it would be preferable to have an interval of at least 12 months before its actual starting date, rather than the six months provided in the Treaty, and the Commission and the Council now seem to appreciate this.

The basket ECU

One of the EMI's tasks will be to 'facilitate the use of the ECU and oversee its development, including the smooth functioning of the ECU clearing system' (*EMI Statute*, Article 4.1). Its role in this connection, as with policy, will be advisory only. It is not required to promote the ECU; rather, to put it on a more equal footing with other currencies.[13] In the EMU IGC some Member States tried to give the EMI a more positive role in relation to the ECU, but this was successfully resisted by Germany and the Netherlands, to whom any suggestion of adopting a parallel currency approach to EMU was unacceptable.

The basket ECU developed quite successfully in Stage I as a specialized investment vehicle for sophisticated investors and borrowers. There is a range of instruments in financial markets denominated in ECUs; several central banks use them in their management of official foreign-exchange reserves; and they have become a significant borrowing medium for governments in some Member States, notably France, Italy and the UK. But the importance of the ECU in the international capital markets is still fairly small. At the end of 1993 ECU-denominated bonds comprised just under 5% by value of the outstanding total of bonds issued by OECD residents on the international markets (see Bank for International Settlements 1994, p. 108); the proportion was much smaller if local currency issues on domestic markets were included. The same is true of the ECU's role as a monetary asset. It has been estimated that ECU-denominated deposits (including interbank deposits, in which ECUs are heavily concentrated) accounted for some 3½% of all M3-type deposits of EC banks (i.e. 'broad money') at the end of 1989, and the overall change since is unlikely to have been large (Bishop 1991a). Only just over 1% of all expenditure on goods and services within the EC is currently settled in ECUs. The ECU thus has significant uses as a specialized investment asset but not as a form of general liquidity or a commercial transactions medium.

Some supporters of the ECU as the future European currency believed before Maastricht that it could provide a market-based route to EMU, and with that in mind they advocated its promotion as a parallel currency in

Stage II. The hard ECU proposed by the UK was one such scheme, but there were others with less emphasis on price stability. Had a parallel currency approach found favour, it would have been important to provide for the EMI to promote the ECU as one of its key tasks, involving taking over its issuance and management from the group of banks which have played the key role in developing the 'private' ECU. But with its rejection, the case for an enhanced role for the ECU in transition disappeared, as did any need for the EMI to take operational responsibility for it.[14]

In some respects the basket ECU's existence will complicate the move to Stage III, given that it was agreed at Maastricht to denominate the new currency in ECU and, implicitly, to call it the 'ecu', notwithstanding German opposition.[15] However expedient this may be politically (outside Germany), there was no economic logic to it. Problems will arise because the new currency, when it is finally launched, will be fundamentally different from the basket ECU. It will be 'a currency in its own right' as the Treaty says, i.e. an independent currency, not a mere unit of account like the existing official ECU, or a 'derivative' asset, whose value derives from the willingness of private-sector institutions to convert it into baskets of national currencies, like the private ECU. Even though the basket ECU will cease to exist officially when Stage III starts, private agents may still calculate it. There could therefore be a problem for contracts denominated in basket ECU which mature in Stage III, because unless all the basket's component currencies join EMU the value of the new ECU will probably diverge from it, possibly substantially. Conflicts could then arise over the value on conversion of ECU contracts, and interest rates thereon. Ideally, these could be avoided in Stage II by the insertion of appropriate contingency clauses in new contracts, and the Commission have offered guidance on this. But disputes could arise over the interpretation of long-term contracts entered into before these concerns surfaced, and these may have to be settled in the courts unless governments are prepared to pass retrospective legislation. The EMI and the Commission will need to give further, early, consideration to these problems, along with corresponding questions relating to conversion of contracts denominated in national currency into the new currency.

Conclusions

The transition to EMU raises problems hardly less severe than EMU itself. Given that EMU could involve serious adjustment costs for some States, it was sensible to set objective tests of suitability for membership, which some may pass and others fail. As many observers have pointed out, this creates the prospect of a multi-speed move to EMU: the Community cannot expect to move forward together as its founders might have wished. But at least the Treaty set the same tests for all Member States, and all have agreed on what the tests should be.

The convergence criteria have attracted heavy criticism, particularly in relation to the arbitrariness of the fiscal criterion and the ambiguity and questionable relevance, especially in the light of subsequent events, of the exchange-rate criterion. More fundamentally, the Treaty's virtual neglect of real economic factors is a concern for economists. Some of these worries could be addressed in the course of decision-making and passage of secondary legislation under the Treaty, given the political will. Among priorities is the clarification by the Council of the exchange-rate criterion so that all involved know what is meant by 'the normal fluctuation margins' of the ERM. Preferably the markets should be reassured that a return to narrow bands is not contemplated. Other priorities include the development of supplementary, if informal, tests for competitiveness and labour-market flexibility, and their application in the convergence assessments.

On the basis of the main criteria as they stand, despite allowing some limited scope for interpretation of the fiscal and exchange-rate criteria, and assuming the currency turbulence of spring 1995 proves temporary, the economic forecasts suggest that the EU with its enlarged membership will be short of the eligible majority required in 1996 for Stage III to start in 1997, especially if the Danish exemption is maintained. Fiscal and exchange-rate risks at present go, if anything, in the direction of fewer States meeting the criteria in the near future, although the result could conceivably tilt the other way if fiscal performance is somewhat better than forecast in several States. The Council at head of State or government level would presumably endorse an ECOFIN recommendation against an early Stage III when the time for formal decisions comes, bearing in mind wider economic worries and political concerns about cohesion.

The clear prospect now is that EMU will commence in 1999, when perhaps six to seven or more willing States seem likely to qualify. Assuming no major unforeseen economic and political shocks, no downturn into new recession, and a smooth end to the current instability among the EC currencies, the balance of probabilities is that Stage III of EMU will start for about half the Member States by around the end of the century, when there will be no formal requirements for a majority, or for an assessment of 'appropriateness'.

The EMI will play an important part in the transition by supporting policies aimed at convergence, and by making technical preparations for Stage III. Even though its policy role is advisory only, its advice will be increasingly heeded because it will be influential in judgments about eligibility, and it will be perceived increasingly as the ECB-in-waiting as Stage III approaches. Its thinking on monetary instruments and procedures will be formative in determining the operational features which will be important for banks and other financial institutions affected by Stage III: although the EMI cannot insist on the adoption of its chosen arrangements, its successor, the ECB, will be able to do so for would-be participants. The EMI will also be influential in planning the introduction of the single currency, and one of its early tasks should be to set out a timetable for conversion, taking account of the Commission's deliberations in this field and clarifying unresolved question about the coexistence of the new ECU with national currencies.

The EMI's task in relation to the basket ECU in Stage II is advisory only, and fairly subsidiary. The rejection of the parallel currency route to EMU meant that the ECU would not play an important part in the transition. The new currency will be a different form of money from the basket ECU, and familiarity with the latter will not be particularly helpful to economic agents as they convert to the new currency.

Chapter 8

The anatomy of Stage III

This chapter discusses key features of the Treaty blueprint for Stage III: the move from fixed exchange-rates to the single currency; the role and status of the ECB; the separation of monetary policy from other areas of policy; and the conduct of the single monetary policy. Consideration is given to possible modifications and to the clarification of certain outstanding issues. Inevitably this entails going beyond pure economics into issues of political economy.

Conversion to the single currency

Although the Delors Report stopped short of pronouncing a single currency essential to EMU, it was 'a natural and desirable further development of the monetary union' and should replace national currencies 'as soon as possible after the locking of parities' (Committee for the Study of Economic and Monetary Union 1989, p. 19). As well as eliminating currency conversion costs and giving the Community's currency a global presence, it would facilitate 'the monetary management of the Community' and clearly demonstrate the irreversibility of EMU. These arguments were accepted in the EMU ICG and the Treaty provides for the 'rapid introduction of the ECU as the single currency' of participating States (*Treaty*, Article 109l.4). However, no timetable was set and little was said about factors governing the move, except that the Council should take the 'necessary measures' (on a proposal from the Commission, and with the advice of the ECB).

As seen in Chapter 5, the introduction of the single currency will take time, perhaps five years; but serious preparations are unlikely to start until governments and business are convinced that Stage III will actually happen and their countries will participate, which can only be shortly before Stage III starts. Some commentators see a 'Catch 22' dilemma arising here, but a problem will arise only if full conversion has to occur soon after the start of Stage III. Unfortunately the Treaty is ambiguous on this timing question. There is no requirement for the ECB to issue ECU notes or other liabilities from the first day, or for commercial banks to offer ECU deposits; the relevant article simply states that 'the ECU will become a currency in its own right' when Stage III starts (ibid.).[1] However, there are (basket) ECU deposits and securities in the market, and the market's expectation is that they will be redominated in 'new' ECU at par when Stage III starts, and convertible at par when they mature – although the Treaty does not state this explicitly.

The Council's decisions on the single currency's introduction will be by unanimity of participating States, so laggards will be in a position to delay change if they are not ready. Although there will be practical advantages from a simultaneous move, some States may be allowed to move before others. Commercial banks may be pressed by their customers to issue deposits denominated in the new currency as soon as Stage III starts, but will be reluctant to do so without ESCB permission, for normal banking prudence suggests that they will wish to be sure of converting national currency into ECU notes or deposits at the ESCB at the 'irrevocably fixed rate' if they issue ECU liabilities at that rate, whereas there is no guarantee of official convertibility in the Treaty. There are unresolved questions here which ought to be clarified.

However the Treaty is interpreted in this respect, the economic arguments do not amount to a strong case for conversion early in Stage III, and it is arguable that it could be postponed for a number of years, perhaps even indefinitely. As explained in Chapter 5, the long-run economic benefits offered by the single currency (beyond those offered by 'irrevocably' fixed exchange rates) are likely to be modest, whereas the costs and disruption of introducing the new currency will be appreciable even though once-for-all. More importantly, the single currency's benefits for 'monetary management' claimed by the Delors Committee are debatable. They were not spelled out, but presumably relate to the instability of quasi-fixed exchange-rate systems in conditions of high international capital mobility, as witnessed in the ERM crisis of 1992–3. But the regime in Stage III will be crucially different, in that there will be a *single monetary policy* administered by a central monetary institution with legal undertakings to maintain fixed rates in all circumstances. Underpinning these commitments will be the ECB's exclusive ability, in effect, to create and withdraw national moneys at will, giving it unlimited power to intervene in foreign-exchange markets if needed. Participants will have abandoned all possibility of pursuing separate monetary policies, short of a new treaty which would have to be agreed by all – or of reneging on the existing treaty.

Furthermore, exchange-rate fixity under EMU will not depend primarily on market intervention. As Kenen has shown, cross-border transactions within the union will be cleared automatically at the 'irrevocably fixed' exchange rates through inter-central bank transfers on the books of the ESCB, much as payments between Federal Reserve Districts in the USA are cleared through the Federal Reserve System (Kenen 1992, Chapter 3). This will require certain preparatory steps: balance sheets of the ECB and ESCB central banks should be denominated in ECU; commercial banks should hold operating balances in ECU with their national central bank; there should be an EMU-wide 'ECB Funds' market (i.e. interbank market for balances held with the ESCB); and governments should attach 'ECU endorsements' (guarantees of ECU value) to all their marketable debt instruments, and similar endorsements should be attached to all private-sector paper dealt in by the ESCB. Preferably, there should also be unified markets for all securities bearing ECU endorsements, and the payments systems of all participating States should be made fully compatible and accessible to all commercial banks in EMU, at least at the wholesale level.[2] The key requirement is that each participating central bank will be ready to swap its national currency for ECU or currencies of other ESCB countries at par, without limit and without margins or commissions.

Markets in national currencies will continue so long as the separate currencies exist, because residents of EMU will need to buy and sell third currencies, and speculative pressures could emerge there if expectations of parity changes developed, but that would happen only if doubts arose about the ECB's commitment to exchange-rate fixity. Admittedly it could come into question in extreme circumstances, if some governments attempted to take advantage of freedom from exchange-rate pressures to run large fiscal deficits, which could create financial problems for EMU, as will be seen below. But provided there are effective arrangements for limiting deficits and for forcing a government into insolvency if its deficit ceases to be financeable from market sources, the ECB need not suspend its commitments and there need be no consequences in the foreign-exchange markets.

There may be questions about the efficacy of the fiscal rules, as will be seen below, and if fiscal discipline were seen not to be working, the ECB's commitment to fixed exchange rates could come under pressure. But similar problems could arise after full conversion to a single currency. There would then be no markets in national currencies, and so no speculation in them, but currency areas can be dismantled, as shown by experience in the former Czechoslovakia, Yugoslavia and Soviet Union, all of which have seen relatively speedy introduction of new regional currencies (Melliss and Cornelius 1994). Ireland's departure from the UK monetary area is another example of smooth disengagement. Although the breakup of a monetary union may bring economic disruption, especially in regions intent on exploiting new-found monetary sovereignty, it is not technically impossible. Even with a single currency, markets will know that EMU is not absolutely irreversible, and large capital outflows could be expected from States whose allegiance to it became seriously in doubt because they found its disciplines too demanding. In so far as the single currency meant greater political commitment to EMU, the possibility of eventual break-up might then seem more remote, but it could not be exorcised for all time. A single currency would not protect the integrity of EMU if participating governments were unwilling to obey, and collectively enforce, sensible fiscal rules.

Establishment of the ESCB-based clearing arrangements envisaged by Kenen should not be unduly difficult or time-consuming given the political will, and cooperation by banks and other financial institutions. Denomination of ECB and participating central-bank balance sheets in ECUs could be done quickly,[3] as could attachment of ECU guarantees to government and eligible commercial paper. Establishment of an efficient ECB funds market and unified markets for ECU-endorsed securities would take longer, as would the build-up of adequate holdings by commercial banks. The six months implied in the Treaty might not be long enough for the necessary market adaptations. Kenen suggests allowing a year between the decision to commence Stage III (when the ECB will be established), and its actual starting date, and this now seems to be accepted by the Council.

As the practical problems of adopting the single currency loom larger, public opinion in candidate States may harden in favour of retaining national currencies for a lengthy period in Stage III. Moreover retention of national currencies is likelier if the initial move to Stage III involves a minority of States, since adoption of the ECU as common *numeraire* will seem less appropriate the fewer national currencies are involved. A small EMU led by Germany is likely to be unenthusiastic about converting to the ECU, given German attachment to the D-mark and mistrust of the basket ECU. There will be fewer market doubts about the permanence of fixed exchange rates if control over monetary policy is seen to pass to an ECB encompassing only convergent, low-inflation currencies.

Technical and 'political economy' considerations thus suggest that there will be a gap of at least several years between the start of Stage III and the full changeover to the new currency. The conversion could occur in a sequence of discrete phases, starting with the adoption of the new currency for all internal accounting purposes by the banking system in participating States (including the ECB and ESCB central banks); moving quickly to the development of an EMU-wide interbank market in ECB funds, denominated in ECUs, together with the associated steps outlined by Kenen; then a phase in which commercial firms switch to ECU accounting and use for invoicing and payments on a voluntary basis; and finally to a 'big bang' replacement of national currency deposits, notes and coin by ECUs which would involve everyone, including households and small firms.[4] Around five years or more might be needed for the entire changeover, including preliminary planning and public education. Assuming that major banks would make few serious preparations before the decisions to move to Stage III, national currencies might continue in use for at least four to five years after its start, but this should not create problems for EMU if governments are seen to be firmly committed to the Treaty.

The European Central Bank

It is widely recognized that the ECB will have a singleness of purpose and independence from political interference second to none among central banks. Maintenance of price stability is stated unequivocally to be its 'primary objective' (*Treaty*, Article 105; *Statute*, Article 2). Although it will have a duty to support 'the general economic policies in the Community' – whose objectives include non-inflationary growth, convergence of economic performance and a high level of employment and of social protection (*Treaty*, Article 2) – this must be 'without prejudice to the objective of price stability'. When carrying out its duties neither the ECB nor an ESCB central bank may seek or take instructions from any other body; and Community institutions and governments of Member States must respect this principle (*Treaty*, Article 107; *Statute*, Article 7).

The arrangements for the ECB's decision-making bodies underline its independence. The members of the Executive Board, which will run it on

113

a day-to-day basis, will have (non-renewable) eight-year terms and can be dismissed only for extreme personal incapacity or misdemeanour. They will be employed full-time and may have no other occupation. They will be appointed by common accord of the European Council on a recommendation from the (ECOFIN) Council, which must consult the European Parliament and the ESCB Governing Council but need not follow their advice. The Governing Council's other members, the governors of participating central banks, may be appointed under their existing procedures (usually by their national governments), but they will have minimum (renewable) five-year terms, and they will be as hard to dismiss as Executive Board members.

As a corollary of the ECB's strong independence, its accountability will be very weak. Although it must report publicly at least quarterly, and issue a consolidated financial statement weekly, its proceedings will be confidential. It must address an annual report on its activities to the EU institutions, and the ECB president must present the report to the Council and Parliament, which may debate it but have no powers to change policy. The president of the ECOFIN Council and a member of the Commission may participate in meetings of the ECB Governing Council, and may 'submit a motion for its deliberation', but not vote. The ECB president or other Board members may be heard by competent committees of the European Parliament, at its request or on their own initiative, but they need not accept the committees' views or anyone else's.

It is unclear how far national central-bank governors will be accountable in their own jurisdictions in Stage III. The Statute does not bar them from appearing before their respective parliamentary committees, but the strong prohibition on taking instructions from other bodies suggests that they could not be *required* to attend (unlike the position now in the UK). Although it might seem unlikely that governors would refuse their parliaments' requests for hearings, they could object to discussing policy details on confidentiality grounds.[5]

ECB accountability is specially weak in that neither the European Parliament nor the Council can change its main powers and duties. The Council can amend the Statute on certain administrative and financial matters, and on the detailed scope of ECB business, and some of these amendments would be subject to European parliamentary assent (*Treaty*, Article 106.5). But (except in the area of prudential supervision) ECB objectives and tasks can be changed only by amending the Treaty or protocols, a far from quick or easy process:

The extent of the delegated power given to the ECB is all the more remarkable in that it is virtually irreversible. To reverse the transfer of power would require an amendment of the Treaty, to be ratified with the consent of the legislatures of all Member States. (Dunnett 1994, p. 144)

Thus the ECB will not be subject to long-range guidance from the political authorities such as is practised in most democracies. Maastricht-style accountability merely means reporting and hearing reactions; it has no connotation of stewardship. The Council will have some influence through its right to appoint Executive Board members, but the non-renewability of their terms means that they will have little incentive to take the Council's views into account after appointment. Even the Bundesbank, generally acknowledged to be one of the most independent of central banks, albeit in its special area of competence, is subject to reform of its powers and objectives by the German parliament, which could change them by amending the Bundesbank Act. A similar situation exists in the USA, where in addition the Federal Reserve Board must promote plural goals, between which it must strike a balance acceptable to the administration and Congress. The latter is also true of the newly independent Banque de France. Although its constitution in 1993 was modelled closely on the ECB blueprint in many respects, a notable exception can be found in its policy mandate: although required to formulate and implement monetary policy with the aim of ensuring price stability, it must do so 'dans le cadre de la politique économique générale du Gouvernement' (Banque de France 1993, Article premier). Thus the French statute does not require price stability to take precedence over other economic objectives.

There are also major differences between the ECB blueprint and the form of central banking independence adopted some years ago in New Zealand. In that approach there is a quantitative inflation target, chosen jointly by government and central bank, over which the government retains a temporary override which it may exercise if circumstances change; and the Governor may be dismissed for failing to meet the target. The New Zealand approach has been seen as an innovative attempt to create operational autonomy for the central bank through a contractual relationship with government. The publication of an explicit target facilitates accountability, making it easier to judge whether the central bank is meeting its objective. There are now comparable arrangements in Australia and Canada, but no counterpart in the Maastricht blueprint.

The closeness of the ECB design to the Bundesbank model reflects a number of factors: wide acceptance of the superiority of the German record on inflation and growth over the past thirty years; the suitability of the federal central banking model for the EC's situation, comprising a group of independent States with relatively weak central institutions, not well placed to exercise firm accountability; and the vital importance attached by other Member States to German participation in EMU. Opinions nevertheless differ on these issues. The Bundesbank strongly supports the Maastricht model, as is evident from many presidential speeches (for example, Schlesinger 1993; Tietmeyer 1994). The Commission advocates full legal independence for the ECB in order to create credibility in the absence of reputation. Some economists are inclined to agree, for example Gros and Thygesen (1992), who believe the ECB needs more independence than the Bundesbank because public opinion is so heavily behind the latter, whereas without legal protection for the ECB there would be few checks on meddling by the Council. Others take a different view, believing that the blueprint goes too far in sacrificing long-term accountability (Williamson 1993c; Kenen 1995a, p. 42).

The issues here are inherently difficult to resolve because, other things being equal, there is likely to be a tradeoff between independence and accountability, which must depend somewhat on national circumstances and history. As Guitian (1995) has argued, the German model, which preserves discretion entirely for the central bank, may be more suitable in economies where there is a history of hyperinflation which has entered the public psyche, and where the wish to constrain the powers of central government has played a large role in recent political history; whereas the New Zealand model of checks and balances may be more suitable in economies where there is a stronger tradition of public economic awareness and debate, and where the financial markets play a major disciplinary and public information role.[6]

Economists tend to see the setting of a *quantitative target for inflation*, whether jointly by government and central bank, or by the central bank after consultation with government, as essential for effective accountability; for example Fischer (1994), in the context of UK reform. Goodhart (1992a) makes the corresponding recommendation for the ECB, and continental economists such as Neumann (1991) and Giovannini (1993) make similar recommendations.

Mainstream British thinking now favours an explicit inflation target, following the policy moves in that direction after sterling left the ERM. In its recent report on the role of the Bank of England, the UK Treasury

Select Committee recommended a version of central banking independence nearer to the New Zealand than the Maastricht model, while seeing accountability working through Parliament rather than the Treasury (Treasury and Civil Service Select Committee 1993, para. 80). A similar conclusion for the UK was reached by an independent 'high-level' panel chaired by Lord Roll, which emphasized the importance of transparency, monitoring and accountability in the central bank's role. They too favoured an explicit, statutory inflation target, although it should be set on the Bank's responsibility only, and the government override should be strictly temporary (Roll Committee 1993). Neither the Select Committee nor the Roll Committee recommended legal sanctions to reinforce accountability, being content to rely on the force of public criticism in the course of parliamentary surveillance.[7] However, both endorsed, if only implicitly, Parliament's right to change the central bank's basic objectives and duties, and hence the exercise of long-range accountability.

The separateness of monetary policy

EMU as envisaged at Maastricht requires the total separation of monetary policy from other policies. This is the accepted situation in countries where an independent central bank is well established, as in Germany, but it would be a new experience in countries where government has traditionally retained ultimate responsibility for all branches of macroeconomic policy, including France and the UK among many others. In principle, conflicts could arise in relation to exchange-rate policy and fiscal policy.

Exchange-rate policy

It is a commonplace of economics that currency exchange rates and relative rates of domestic inflation are interdependent and that in the long run, given freedom of international capital flows, they must adjust to match each other. One concern about the Maastricht blueprint has been that ECOFIN may adopt an (external) exchange-rate policy in Stage III which is inconsistent with the ECB's price-stability objective, given inflation elsewhere, and oblige the ECB to take action which jeopardizes its objective. The possibility arises because, although the ECB will be in charge of day-to-day management of the ECU's exchange rate, and over the bulk of participants' foreign-exchange reserves, ECOFIN will have the right to enter into international agreements involving the single currency, or alternatively formulate 'general orientations' for its exchange rate

(*Treaty*, Article 109). This was a compromise in the IGC reflecting the fact that governments have usually regarded exchange-rate policy as their prerogative and that despite EMU they are not ready to abandon it entirely.

Purists see this division of responsibility for monetary and exchange-rate policy as illogical and potentially damaging (Begg et al. 1991). German experience at the time of reunification provided a notable illustration. There was then a sharp disagreement between the FRG government and the Bundesbank over the exchange rate at which Ostmark balances would be converted into D-marks, and the central bank was overruled, with consequences that are widely thought to have been damaging for monetary policy in Germany and, subsequently, elsewhere in the ERM. Supporters of central banking autonomy insist that the central bank must be free to devote all its policy instruments to its monetary policy objective (Roll Committee 1993).

However, this policy separation is unlikely to be troublesome in practice unless circumstances greatly change. First, formal agreements pegging the new ECU to other major currencies will continue to be out of fashion in a world where the G-3 currencies are accustomed to managed floating.[8] Secondly, the Treaty wording is strongly protective of the ECB: action by the Council would have to be on a recommendation from the Commission or the ECB, would require unanimity, and would be after consultation with the ECB 'in an endeavour to reach a consensus consistent with the objective of price stability' (*Treaty*, Article 109). Thirdly, although ECOFIN might wish to issue 'general orientations' in support of *informal* agreements involving the dollar and yen, they would have to be 'without prejudice to the primary objective of the ESCB to maintain price stability' (ibid.) They would thus not be binding, and it would be for the ECB to decide whether they conflicted with its primary objective; if so it could quietly ignore them. Finally, participating governments would be anxious to make EMU work and would hardly be likely to enter collective commitments which challenged the ECB's authority, even though some might have national objectives pulling in a different direction.

Fiscal policy
The separation of responsibilities for monetary and fiscal policy in Stage III raises the possibility that the 'policy mix' may become unbalanced. This could happen if a number of participating countries, or a single large country, use the freedom from external constraints offered by EMU to pursue chronically expansionary fiscal policies.[9] Their ability to do so under EMU will be enhanced because, without exchange-rate risk, dif-

ferent governments' bonds will be closer substitutes for one another than now, and this will decrease the sensitivity of the interest rates faced by individual governments to their borrowing record. Moreover the incentives to do so may be stronger under EMU, since structural problems are likely to be more exposed then. Persistent fiscal deficits could generate damaging 'spillover' effects for other participants, ultimately (in the face of the ECB's non-accommodating monetary policy) raising real interest rates throughout EMU, notwithstanding open international capital markets – either through disturbing the global balance of savings and investment, or through an increase in the risk premium on the ECU, reflecting uncertainty about future inflation. Alternatively or in addition, the ECU would tend to appreciate in real terms (recalling US experience in the early 1980s). Both effects would mean crowding out of investment and, in time, adverse effects on capacity and output across the group. If such policies were carried to extremes, the solvency of heavily indebted governments would sooner or later come into question, and this might create additional spillover effects in the form of a general financial crisis threatening financial institutions across EMU.

Some economists have pointed to the possibility of *cumulative* instability if monetary and fiscal policies are conducted independently in EMU (Meade and Weale 1992). A damaging spiral might develop in which, for example, an initial cost-push stimulus leads to monetary policy tightening by the ECB, which induces governments to raise tax rates in an effort to reverse a rise in their budget deficits (through the fiscal stabilizers), which in turn generates further cost-push pressure and thence more monetary tightening, etc. This instability could be avoided if treasuries and central banks cooperated in pursuit of agreed targets for inflation and activity.

Such problems were foreseen by the Delors Committee and led it to recommend both a strengthening of fiscal policy coordination and mandatory fiscal rules (Committee for the Study of Economic and Monetary Union 1989, pp. 23–4). However, the Treaty paid scant attention to policy coordination, which is to remain an indicative exercise based on 'guidelines'; and although it followed the Delors advice in introducing fiscal constraints, they have a number of drawbacks. The 'no monetary financing' rule may help to protect the ECB's monetary policy freedom, but it will not necessarily constrain fiscal deficits, since the ECB may have to purchase government debt on secondary markets to prevent interest rates from rising, and the ECU from appreciating, in the event of excessive deficits (Kenen 1995a, Chapter 2). And the 'no bailout' rule, even if rigorously applied, will not be effective if markets price risk inefficiently and charge premia which are insufficient to deter governments (relying on their extensive taxation powers) from heavy debt accumulation, as has happened in the past – for example in the Latin American debt crises of the early 1980s. If so, borrowing may continue until markets eventually perceive national debt burdens to be unsustainable, at which point there might be a financial crisis which the ECB could not contain without relaxing policy and jeopardizing price stability.

The rules on *excessive deficits* promise better protection against an unbalanced policy mix, even though they focus on national actions only, and address problems of solvency rather than coordination (Kenen 1995a, p. 93). But they too have weaknesses. They are arbitrary, making no allowance for the general fiscal position across participants as a whole, or for the economic cycle, or shocks of any kind. There can be some flexibility in their interpretation by the Council: a deficit may be allowable if 'the excess over the reference value is only exceptional and temporary and the deficit remains close to the reference value' (*Treaty*, Article 104c.2) – the reference value being 3% of GDP. But the scope for judgment here will be small, because deficits have to be 'close' to the reference value whatever allowance is made. There is more room for flexibility on the *debt* ratio, which may exceed its reference value (60% of GDP) if 'the ratio is sufficiently diminishing and approaching the reference value at a satisfactory pace', with no requirement for closeness (ibid.). However, a finding of an excessive *deficit* will be sufficient to trigger disciplinary proceedings in Stage III.

A related concern is that in Stage III, unlike Stage II where the threat of exclusion from EMU is powerful, the Treaty sanctions against excessive deficits may be ineffective. Disciplinary action on an ascending scale is provided for, starting with a confidential recommendation from the Council to the government concerned and moving on to publication in the event of non-compliance, with an assessment of the scale of fiscal action needed; and thence, in Stage III, to suspension of lending by the European Investment Bank to the country concerned, imposition of a 'non-interest-bearing deposit' and ultimately 'fines of an appropriate size' (Article 104c.11). However, the Council may choose not to take such steps for political reasons, and there is no indication of the guiding factors.

The efficacy of the excessive-deficit procedure is thus rather unpredictable. In some cases, the threat of public censure by the Community coupled with downgrading of the borrower's credit rating may be enough to secure compliance; in others, governments set on expansion may believe these penalties to be a price worth paying for fiscal freedom, and some may be prepared to risk suspension of EIB lending, and even EC deposits and fines.[10] The arbitrariness of the fiscal limits may encourage governments to ignore them, since it could induce the European Court to take a lenient view if it were asked to adjudicate in a dispute over the procedure.

Concerns of this kind have led to calls for a strengthening of fiscal policy coordination in EMU, failing a substantial enlargement of the Community budget – a step which the McDougall Report held necessary for successful monetary union (MacDougall 1977). Such concerns are not confined to economists; they are shared by, among others, central bankers, for example, ex-Bundesbank president Pöhl, who chaired the EC governors' committee when it drafted the ESCB Statute, and who argued that 'a substantial transfer of authority will also be necessary in the field of fiscal policy' (Appendix to the Delors Report, p. 136). The Delors Committee itself stressed that 'the arrangements in the budgetary field should enable the Community to conduct a coherent mix of fiscal and monetary policies' (p. 24) and recommended the development of 'binding rules and procedures for budgetary policy' involving not only limits on deficits and a no-monetary-financing rule but also 'the definition of the overall stance of fiscal policy over the medium term, including the size and financing of the aggregate budgetary balance, comprising both the national and the Community positions' (p. 28).

It should be possible to move towards the Delors Committee's recommendation by modifying the excessive-deficit procedure without weakening its basic thrust. This might be done by setting a lower deficit figure as the cyclical average objective, but making some allowance for cyclical factors in judging whether deficits are excessive (Crockett 1994, p. 179). In a simple approach, the reference value for deficits could be averaged over a run of years (perhaps five). Any impression that constraints were being weakened could be countered by setting the reference value for the medium term at, say, 2% of GDP rather than 3% – or even at zero, as Crockett has suggested; and perhaps by making the approach forward-looking, which could be done by including (Commission) forecasts in the reference period. A more ambitious approach would cyclically adjust the reference values, but cyclical adjustment is an inexact technique which is quite sensitive to the assumptions made, and might be better kept as a supplementary tool of analysis.

Another step in the Delors direction would be to introduce quantitative limits for the Community's *combined* fiscal deficit (as a percentage of aggregate GDP), again averaged over the medium term, and apply them as additional criteria in assessing national deficits.[11] The EU limit might be the same as that for an individual State, or lower, but not higher. A finding that the EU's combined deficit exceeded, or was forecast to exceed, its reference value would be taken as a *prima facie* signal that individual States' deficits were too high, and the Council would be required to take this into account in assessing individual deficits. There should be no presumption that equiproportionate reductions would be required in all States' deficits, for this could mean rewarding fiscal laxity: the Council would have scope to judge the size of correction required from individual States. The point of the combined limit is that it would introduce a systematic element of coordination into the Council's fiscal judgments. It could be ECOFIN's task in consultation perhaps with the *General* Council of the ECB (including non-participants in EMU) to set the limit and review it periodically.

Modifications of this kind could also assist the implementation of sanctions, in that less arbitrary fiscal limits would make the imposition of penalties more credible. Ways might also be found of making the sanctions themselves more transparent and predictable. For example, an explicit sliding scale could be adopted for deposits and fines which depended on the size of the 'deficit reduction which is judged necessary by the Council'. In recalcitrant cases the penalty could rise to equal the necessary reduction. But any such toughening should depend on modifying the rules as outlined above.

The single monetary policy

The Treaty says very little about the single monetary policy, beyond endowing the ECB with the basic powers to conduct it, and leaving the preparation of instruments and procedures to the EMI. Yet there are more than just technical issues at stake.

Intermediate targets

The ECB is likely to adopt *intermediate* targets to guide its policy. If so, the focus will doubtless be on domestic rather than external targets, given that EMU will comprise a larger and less open market than its members individually. This will be an important change of focus for ERM central banks, which still regard the exchange rate as their principal target – except for Germany, which as the ERM anchor country has consistently pursued a domestically oriented policy.

The Bundesbank's approach over the years has been to focus primarily on the behaviour of a domestic monetary aggregate, formerly 'central bank money' and latterly 'broad money' (M3), as Issing (1992) has set out. There are various possible alternatives, including narrower aggregates such as 'base money' (notes and coin and bankers' balances at the central bank) or 'narrow money' (M1); or some measure of aggregate nominal incomes or expenditure (GDP or GNP at current prices); or even some (leading) measure of inflation itself, as adopted in a growing number of countries, including Canada, Finland, New Zealand, Spain, Sweden and the UK. All have their pros and cons as intermediate targets.[12] Monetary aggregates are timelier and less subject to measurement error or revision than national-accounts aggregates; and they are more amenable to control by the central bank, even if it confines itself to using market-based techniques. Inflation reacts to monetary policy action with a long lag, probably of the order of two years or more in most States, which means its use as a target creates a risk of policy-overshooting. The fact that the Germans with their successful inflation record continue to use monetary aggregates is a strong argument in their favour. However, even in Germany the stability of the relationship between M3 and inflation has come into question in recent years, increasingly since reunification.

There will doubtless be strong advocacy from the Bundesbank of M3 or some related measure of broad money as an intermediate target (Deutsche Bundesbank 1993), and this approach may attract support from other central banks, a number of which are accustomed to using monetary aggregates as supplementary targets. On this view the ECB, as a new and untried institution, ought to give clear guidance to the markets on how it will conduct policy, and pre-set targets should boost credibility (Issing 1994). But there are objections. Past relationships between money, incomes and inflation may be no guide to the future, after the major regime change. Furthermore the financial liberalization and competition promoted by the Single Market will disturb established monetary relationships in continental economies, as happened earlier in 'Anglo-Saxon' ones; indeed it is already happening on the continent, not least in Germany. As competition develops in hitherto cartelized banking systems there, the interest rates paid on monetary assets will behave more like those on non-monetary assets (as has happened in the UK since the banking liberalizations of the 1970s and early 1980s), and it will be harder for central banks to influence the *difference* in the yields on money and competing assets by managing the *general level* of (short-term) interest rates, which is the principal means by which they seek to control money in market-based regimes.

A counterargument is that the instability noted in national money–inflation relationships since the early 1980s reflects, in part, substitution between EC currencies resulting from the freeing of international capital flows, and this source of instability should disappear when national money stocks are merged under EMU. Research done so far suggests that the demand for 'global ERM' money may be more stable against the usual determinants than national money stocks (Kremers and Lane 1990; Monticelli and Strauss-Kahn 1993). However, the results have been challenged (Barr 1992) and it is too early yet to form a confident view.[13] In any case, the uncertainty about the membership of EMU makes the argument hard to assess.

The Bank of England among others is likely to press for greater flexibility in the use of monetary aggregates, pointing out that the Bundesbank itself has appeared in recent years to pay more attention to underlying inflation than to M3, as the velocity of money circulation in Germany has become less predictable. It would be damaging as well as unnecessary for the ECB to nail its colours to a target that proved to be an unreliable guide to inflation; the huge uncertainties at the start of Stage III therefore point to caution. There are attractions in a flexible approach in which a number of aggregates and leading indicators are monitored, reported and acted upon by the ECB, as the EMI has noted (European Monetary Institute 1995, pp. 73–4). Such an approach would gain, especially in its early experimental stages, from the announcement of an underlying inflation target explicit enough to enable markets to assess the ECB's performance in relation to its basic objective.

Policy instruments and procedures
Whatever the ECB's approach to targetry, its choice of monetary instruments and operating procedures should not be greatly affected. The eventual choice should depend on how financial structures evolve in the meantime, for example the payments infrastructure of Stage III and the nature of financial flows between the ESCB and its customers, particularly governments; but it seems certain that the ECB will use short-term interest rates as its primary instrument of monetary control. Most central banks nowadays rely on their ability to influence interest rates; few if any seek to ration the supply of funds to the banking system through administrative controls, although some keep them in reserve for emergencies. Moreover the ECB is required by the Statute to operate in accordance with 'the principle of an open market economy with free competition, favouring an efficient allocation of resources' (*Statute*, Article 2) and this

clearly means using the price mechanism to influence money and credit.

Although all Member States support this general principle, some central banks are less attached to market-based techniques than others, and some will be more sympathetic to harmonization and centralization than others. The solutions found to these questions will influence the openness and efficiency of the union's banking system, and could greatly affect financial institutions both there and in other centres.

One issue of particular significance is that of *minimum reserve requirements* (MRRs). The ECB will have power to require 'credit institutions established in Member States' to hold minimum reserves with itself or ESCB central banks 'in pursuance of monetary policy objectives' (*Statute*, Article 19).[14] At present MRRs are in force in nine Member States (Germany, France, Italy, Spain, Austria, Finland, Portugal, Ireland and Greece) (European Monetary Institute 1995, Table 16); so there may be majority support for them in EMU. Their purpose is primarily to assist the central bank in managing short-term interest rates in centres where markets for treasury bills and other debt instuments are less deep and liquid than in sophisticated centres. MRRs create a predictable increase in the demand for reserves at the central bank when banks' balance sheets grow in response to demands for money and credit, which it meets on its chosen terms. Since reserves held at the central bank usually pay either no interest or interest at below market rates, there is an incentive on banks to raise their lending rates if their business expands faster than the central bank wishes, and this puts a brake on monetary growth.

Other justifications are also advanced for MRRs. It is sometimes argued that they facilitate monetary control because they provide a stable link between broad money (roughly, the deposit liabilities of the banking system) and reserves of which the central bank is the monopoly supplier. Opponents contest this argument, for example on the ground that banks often keep reserves in excess of the requirement, so that the 'money multiplier' is relatively elastic, and indeed responsive to interest differentials. On this view, MRRs in sophisticated financial markets contribute nothing to monetary control that more flexible control methods cannot achieve, with equivalent consequences for interest rates. But the strongest objection to MRRs which are wholly or partly unremunerated is that they impose, in effect, a discriminatory tax on the banking system. The result is distortion and inefficiency, involving uneconomic disintermediation or diversion of lending to uncontrolled institutions, including offshore branches of domestic banks. For evidence, the experience of extensive disintermediation in Britain during the operation of the Supplementary

Special Deposit scheme in the 1970s is commonly referred to. There is also evidence that MRRs encourage disintermediation in European financial centres, although identification there is complicated because competition between banks and other financial institutions is often also limited by the authorities in other ways, as in the German system.

As financial liberalization has proceeded in European centres in recent years, the case against MRRs has gained support and the rates at which MRRs are imposed have been reduced in States that retain them. The weight of opinion may move further against them before EMU is established. Yet the Bundesbank still appears strongly attached to them (Deutsche Bundesbank 1993) and the prospect remains that non-remunerated MRRs will be adopted in Stage III, at a harmonized rate for all participating banks.[15] Alternatively, the MRR ratio could be set at zero, which is effectively the situation in the UK (where banks must be in balance with the Bank of England at the end of every working day). That would eliminate any tax on banks while offering as much control as could be achieved with positive MRRs. Flexibility could be incorporated by allowing the reserve requirement to be averaged over some period such as a month, as is usual in existing regimes; this would remove the need for high-frequency (e.g. daily) central banking intervention in the money markets, which the ECB will probably wish to avoid, given its hierarchical decision-making structure. A compromise is possible in which the MRR is set at a relatively low ratio to liabilities (perhaps at the 0.5–1.0% currently seen in France) and remunerated at only slightly below a full market rate.[16] This would avoid the worst of the anti-competitive effects, although at some cost (their supporters believe) to their efficacy as control devices.

A more novel solution to the management of interest rates in less sophisticated centres, or where operations in government or private-sector paper are hampered by excessive credit risk, would be for the ECB to issue and deal in its own short-term debt. That would be fully consistent with a market-based approach. It might take time to build up market holdings in sufficient quantities to make such operations effective, but the knowledge that participating central banks and ultimately governments stand behind the ECB should help to make such paper generally acceptable. A problem could be that ECB paper might supplant market holdings of other instruments, and pressure might emerge for the ECB to purchase the latter (in the secondary market), which would recreate problems of credit risk. The technique would therefore need to be used with discretion.

MRRs are just one of a large number of operational questions which will have to be decided before the ECB commences business.[17] Others include methods of *relieving* liquidity shortages (or absorbing surpluses) in the banking system, where the choice is between open market operations (on the initiative of the central bank) and standing facilities such as 'discount window' lending (on the initiative of the banks), with the former likely to be accepted as the predominant technique, as it is more flexible, although less amenable to decentralized operation; the categories of assets and range of counterparties to be dealt with by the ESCB, where there are important issues relating to the desirable degree of harmonization, the extent of acceptable credit risk, and the breadth of access by banks to ESCB credit and dealing facilities; and the distribution of responsibility for money-market and foreign-exchange operations between the ECB and the national central banks. Some of these technical and organizational questions raise matters of wider significance. For example, if unremunerated MRRs are adopted, there is likely to be pressure for arrangements to compensate the banks via other devices, such as the provision by the ECB of a 'base load' of liquidity at below-market rates through quotas to selected banks – on the model of the Bundesbank's discount facility. Any subsidized facility would be hard to reconcile with 'the principle of an open market with free competition', and would tend to create a cartel of privileged banks.

Regarding the division of labour within the ESCB, practical considerations suggest that foreign-exchange operations will be carried out largely by the ECB itself, since rapid decisions may be required from time to time, and a large slice of the ESCB's foreign-exchange reserves will be on the ECB's books; but money-market operations may be delegated to the national central banks, initially at least. There will be a natural inclination for the latter, especially those in less efficient centres, to favour decentralized procedures – MRRs and standing facilities operated locally, rather than open market operations – which promise a wide allocation of business (e.g. in rough proportion to national shares in the ECB's capital). Although the Statute is not specific, it might be interpreted as supporting this kind of approach: 'To the extent deemed possible and appropriate ... the ECB shall have recourse to the national central banks to carry out the operations which form part of the tasks of the ESCB' (*Statute*, Article 12.1, third paragraph). However, efficiency considerations suggest that the ECB should direct its business to centres which offer the all-round best and cheapest service, including markets located outside EMU. It is hard to predict what this would imply for the distribution of ESCB operations. Scale economies in wholesale financial markets suggest that the ECB should in due course develop its business through a relatively small number of efficient and innovative financial centres, rather than spreading them evenly across its national branches, and the ECB should be encouraged to work to this end, pursuing 'evolutionary standardisation', as Kenen (1995a, pp. 66-9) has advocated.[18]

Conclusions

The Maastricht design for Stage III has many strengths, but there are also problems, some of them more than technical. Some features would benefit from clarification, which ought to be possible without Treaty amendment; and some from modification, which would be difficult if it involved changing the Treaty or protocols.

In popular debate on EMU it is often taken for granted that the single currency will replace national currencies at or near the start of Stage III. However, EMU could operate in a stable way with separate national currencies locked together, provided participating governments obey sensible policy rules. The incremental benefits from moving to a single currency are then relatively modest, although eventually positive. The logistical problems of introducing the new currency are likely to create popular pressure for its postponement, but this need not mean postponing EMU altogether. An attractive solution, bearing in mind also the inheritance of the existing (basket) ECU, would be to introduce the new currency in a series of clearly defined and planned stages, with the final stage of conversion taking place as a 'big bang' after banks and the public had completed all necessary preparations. The whole process could take perhaps five to seven years after the key decisions are made. Given the interdependencies involved, between individual banks and between banks and their customers, coordination backed by legal authority would be vital.

Whichever conversion programme seems most feasible, the Treaty provisions relating to the introduction of the new currency should be clarified by the Commission and the EMI as soon as possible, so that all those likely to be concerned know where they stand and can start preparations in good time. This will mean explaining what the ECB itself will do, and expect ESCB central and commercial banks to do, in relation to issuance of ECU banknotes and deposits from Stage III's start. The provisions for the later stages of transition should be adapted to allow more time between the decision to move to Stage III and its actual start.

Regarding the ECB's constitution, it is arguable that the balance struck in the Treaty between independence and accountability allows too much weight to the former. Given the priority attached to price stability in EMU, it was to be expected that the new central bank would be independent of political interference, and seen to be so; but that should not mean exempting it entirely from all processes of democratic control. There is a crucial difference between *ad hoc* interference and long-range guidance. Drawing on other examples of newly independent central banks, ways should be found of bringing democratic authority ultimately to bear if the ECB's performance persistently and significantly misses its objectives; it should not be judge and jury in its own case, however dedicated and competent its top officials.

Bearing in mind the practical difficulties of exercising democratic accountability under EMU because of the EU's confederal nature, improvements might include primarily: the adoption and announcement, by the ECB after consultation with ECOFIN, of a quantitative inflation target or range for the medium term, and its review annually; powers for the European Parliament to approve the appointment of the ECB's president, vice-president and executive directors, on nominations by the Council; and powers for the Council to amend any part of the Treaty and Statute affecting the objectives and functions of the ECB and ESCB, except its price-stability mandate (*Treaty*, Article 105.1; *Statute*, Article 2), on a proposal from the European Parliament. These amendments would clearly mean a significant increase in the powers of the European Parliament. Ideally, consideration should also be given to provision of a *strictly temporary* override of the inflation target in the event of a major external shock, exercisable by ECOFIN subject to European Parliament confirmation; but such a significant departure from the German model would be regarded as dangerous by some, and would in any case be extremely hard to secure.

The retention of fiscal sovereignty in national hands creates important risks for EMU in the form of a bias towards excessively expansionary fiscal policy among governments concerned to ameliorate structural problems exposed by EMU. Safeguards in the form of sensible fiscal rules have a part to play but the rules agreed at Maastricht are likely to constrain unduly the ability of responsible national governments to accommodate shocks and cycles in activity. The rules could be improved by giving the excessive-deficit procedure a medium-term and a pan-EC dimension without weakening its thrust, on lines suggested above; and by making the sanctions under the procedure more explicit and therefore predictable, as also suggested. These modifications could be adopted by (unanimous) decision of the Council, which has power to replace the protocol (*Treaty*, Article 104c.14), without need for Treaty amendment.

On the single monetary policy, there are many questions still to be decided. There will be pressure on the ECB to adopt a domestic monetary aggregate as its principal intermediate target. This could be a useful approach if it is not applied mechanically, bearing in mind the likely instability and unpredictability of money–inflation relationships in Stage III. Other leading indicators of inflation should also be monitored, as well as official and private-sector forecasts of inflation itself; and monetary aggregates should be complemented by a medium-term inflation target, for technical control purposes as well as on the accountability grounds discussed earlier.

When it comes to selecting instruments and procedures for use by the ESCB, there will be pressures for harmonization on the German model because it is believed to have been the most effective. However, circumstances will be different in EMU, and it would be better to select the best features from the various national models and combine them in a coherent system. There will also be pressure to retain as much as possible of the existing monetary operations of central banks which join the ESCB; while understandable, this should be resisted if it conflicts with the efficiency and efficacy of ECB business.

In the area of monetary control, the most problematic issue is likely to be the adoption of minimum reserve ratios for the banking system, but it is doubtful whether they contribute much to monetary control in sophisticated centres, and unless fully remunerated they impose in effect a discriminatory tax on banks, which would detract markedly from EMU's competitiveness. If, despite their disadvantages, MRRs are adopted, the relevant ratio should preferably be zero, averaged over a month; if positive MRRs are insisted on, they should carry interest not far below market rates. In this and other respects, the ECB should adopt instruments and procedures which maximize the efficiency of its operations judged in an overall market context, even if this means concentrating them in a few major centres rather than spreading them evenly among ESCB centres.

Chapter 9

The decisions ahead

It was concluded in Chapter 6 that economic research does not give clear-cut guidance on whether the EU should form a monetary union, or which countries should join. There are likely to be net benefits in the long run, but their size is highly uncertain and the risks will be much greater for some States than others. The decisions ahead will therefore need to take account of the circumstances facing different groups of economies.

An EMU for the 'core'

According to the evidence in Chapter 4 on output composition, trade openness and susceptibility to asymmetric shocks, there is a core group of structurally compatible and integrated economies in the Community which could probably move safely to a monetary union without delay. Germany and the Netherlands have already gone a long way towards doing so, and they could be joined by others without much risk – Luxembourg, Belgium, Denmark (if willing) and Austria – to make an EMU of six countries closely integrated with Germany and similar in terms of economic objectives. There are some grounds for thinking that they could safely be joined by others, notably France and possibly Ireland, but other evidence casts doubt on this. Both economies appear set to meet the Treaty's (nominal) convergence criteria, but real factors are less reassuring. In particular both have high, and seemingly increasing, structural unemployment, suggesting the existence of labour-market rigidities which could create difficulties under EMU. Moreover, Ireland has many features of a 'peripheral' economy (distance from the core's markets, a relatively undeveloped industrial structure, and heavy dependence on trade with the UK). There is therefore a serious question about its readiness for early EMU, although transfers through the structural funds are an important compensating factor in Ireland's case.

Similar reservations can be expressed about Sweden and Finland, which are often held to be strong candidates for EMU. On the unemployment record, both appear to suffer from important labour-market rigidities. In Sweden's case these reflect the well-known problem of high non-wage costs. Sweden admittedly seems very competitive at present in terms of labour costs, but this owes a lot to successive phases of exchange-rate depreciation, allied recently to a slack labour market. Finland's structural problems reflect mainly that economy's heavy past reliance on trade with the Comecon area, the collapse of which necessitated major adjustment in Finnish industry at the end of the 1980s. That process may still have some way to go.

At the other end of the convergence spectrum, there is a group of peripheral, less developed economies which seem clearly unready for EMU, and unlikely to be ready for some time. They comprise Greece, Portugal and Spain, and possibly Italy, although northern Italy is highly developed. Admittedly, Italy's inflation performance and external current account have improved after the lira's depreciation of 1992–3. With the exception of Portugal, all seem to have important labour-market rigidities; and all have had to resort to substantial exchange depreciation in the past few years. Greece and Italy will find it hard to meet the debt criterion by the end of the century without further fiscal cuts, which could plunge them into prolonged recession.

With a core of six States around Germany, plus (tentatively) France, ready for EMU and a 'peripheral' group of three plus (tentatively) Italy not ready, some four States are left in between – Ireland, Finland, Sweden and the UK. All seem only partially integrated with the core group, shown in the UK's case by proneness to asymmetric shocks *vis-à-vis* the core; and all have been driven to periodic depreciation to overcome structural imbalance in recent years. Yet all seem to have a reasonable chance of meeting the main criteria by end-1997 (although the United Kingdom might be required to rejoin the ERM by end-1995); and all seem likely to remain competitive then (within Europe, if not externally), assuming they can control inflation in the meantime. Whether they would be well-advised economically to join EMU by the end of the century is therefore finely balanced; the answer turns, more than for the two other groups, on political-economy judgments.

Institutional issues

On the arguments of Chapter 8, there are two outstanding features of Stage III which should cause Member States to hesitate before joining – the weak accountability of the ECB and the possibility of conflict between the ECB's monetary policy and national fiscal policies.

The rationale for *weak accountability* in EMU is that it is necessary to take monetary policy completely out of the political arena in order to shield it from governments seeking short-term popularity by stimulating the economy excessively and at the wrong times. The counterargument is that unless there is a firm popular consensus on price stability as a policy priority, removal of monetary policy from political influence will sooner or later create serious friction in modern democracies: whereas if that consensus exists, long-range democratic surveillance will not be damaging, and may be beneficial in reinforcing good performance by the ECB and providing transparency in relations between it and the Council.

Citizens of countries with strong democratic traditions and a degree of monetary-policy sovereignty would be entitled to strong misgivings about the ECB's weak accountability, assuming they understood what the Treaty implies. In most Western industrial democracies, with the exception of Germany and Switzerland, the central bank has traditionally been answerable in policy matters to an arm of government, and indirectly via ministers or a government-appointed council to parliament (Swinburne and Castello-Branco 1991, pp. 27–30). In the UK, the Chancellor of the Exchequer, who retains ultimate responsibility for monetary policy, is answerable to Parliament, and could be removed if the government lost a vote of confidence in the House of Commons.[1] As noted earlier, latest expert thinking on the role of the Bank of England prescribes a strengthened form of accountability to Parliament.

It should be possible to bolster ECB accountability without abandoning the Maastricht commitment to price stability or exposing it to short-run political pressures. The modifications suggested in Chapter 8 would make the ECB's policy mandate more transparent and provide an element of long-range democratic surveillance through the European Parliament.[2] Such an extension of the European Parliament's monetary role would increase grassroots interest in the institution and reduce the EU's much criticized 'democratic deficit'.

As seen in Chapter 8, the possibility of *conflict between monetary and fiscal policy* remains a crucial concern in the EMU debate. Two comparatively radical solutions could be envisaged. One would be to relocate

133

a substantial portion of national taxation and public expenditure – perhaps about a fifth – in a central EU budget, resembling more closely the situation in most existing federations. However, this would require a degree of centralization of governmental functions in the EU which is not foreseeable now or for many years to come, if at all. An alternative solution would be to establish a central fiscal authority in EMU with powers to determine national fiscal balances, but leaving tax and expenditure levels for national decision. Such an authority would be a fiscal counterweight to the ECB, with which it would need to consult closely to ensure overall policy consistency. ECOFIN, or a sub-group representing EMU participants, might perform the task; it currently oversees fiscal policy, but cannot set deficits. But giving ECOFIN this power would cut across the prerogatives of national authorities and could hardly be contemplated without a major transfer of fiscal authority from national parliaments to the European Parliament. There would appear to be no greater willingness to cede powers for this purpose than to create a large central budget, even among States which are usually regarded as EMU enthusiasts.

There remains the approach adopted at Maastricht – national fiscal limits enshrined in the excessive-deficit procedure. These have weaknesses but if modifications were introduced as suggested in Chapter 8 to make them more workable and less arbitrary, the prospects of governments' observing them would be enhanced. Admittedly, their observation could not be guaranteed. Short of fiscal centralization, backed by federal-type institutions, nothing could guarantee observance of international fiscal rules by sovereign States.

This does not mean that EMU could not operate effectively without centralized political institutions, but effective operation would depend crucially on the continuing willingness of participating governments to obey sensible fiscal rules. The probability of securing willing acquiescence in fiscal discipline under EMU is a matter for political judgment, which each applicant State ought to make before joining. It should be borne in mind that fiscal responsibility would not rest solely on voluntary intergovernmental cooperation. The market would provide an important deterrent to fiscal excess if the 'no bailout' rule were credible, although satisfactory experience of crunch situations in Stage III might be needed before adequate credibility were established. Reforms to improve the efficiency of market lending to EU governments, such as those recommended by Bishop in the field of prudential supervision, as noted earlier, would help. Participants in EMU would, moreover, know that the Stage

III rules would not be set in stone. Detailed arrangements could evolve through Council decision as experience accumulated, and Treaty amendment would be possible in a subsequent IGC if some key feature were found susceptible to abuse, or worked badly.

More fundamentally, participants would have available to them the ultimate possibility of leaving EMU if things went wrong. Given the nature of currency unions, it would be difficult to expel participating States against their will, for once a common money is established it is hard to stop the citizens of one region from using it. The most that might be done to discipline an uncooperative State, apart from invoking tough sanctions under the excessive-deficit procedure, would be to suspend its central-bank governor's voting rights on the ECB Council, but even this might not suffice to remedy fiscal excess – and there is no provision for it in the Treaty. Equally, however, sovereign States could not be compelled to remain in a monetary union if they objected. Germany (for example) could leave EMU after a period of trial if others were demonstrably not observing the rules – by withdrawing the Bundesbank from the ESCB and re-establishing a separate currency and monetary policy. The political consequences of such a key member's withdrawing would probably be extremely damaging for EMU and the EU, and it would have to be kept as a last resort, but the threat could not be ignored. For these reasons, the argument that fiscal coherence within EMU would inevitably require political union on federal lines is not convincing.

Prospects for the next IGC

It is intended that the IGC due in 1996 will address a wide range of political and institutional issues. Among remits from Maastricht are the EU's security and defence arrangements; the three-pillar construction of the Union (with the possibility of the second two pillars becoming more institutionalized); the respective decision-making roles of the Council, the Parliament and the Commission, and the hierarchy of their various legislative acts. Subsequently other major issues have been added to the agenda: voting rights in the Council, particularly the balance between larger and smaller States; and the size of the Commission, in the context of enlargement.

It was agreed to hold another IGC because some Member States (notably Germany) insisted on a stronger political dimension to monetary integration, in the belief that EMU can only be successful if there is a firm consensus on other policies, especially social and fiscal policies – a view strongly urged by Bundesbank presidents (Tietmeyer 1995). Subsequently a body of opinion has emerged in the ruling CDU/CSU party coalition in Germany which sees a federal-type political union as the primary objective for the EU, with EMU a vital component rather than an end in itself (Schäuble and Lamers 1994). This envisages a small core group of States moving ahead separately towards greater integration of social, foreign and security policies as well as economic policy – to which others could aspire in due course;[3] and a considerable increase in the powers of the European Parliament, which would acquire equal law-making status with the Council as the lower house of a bicameral legislature, with the Commission taking on 'features of a European Government'.

Such radical proposals would be unpalatable for Member States which do not wish to move further towards a centralized system of government and security for the EU – most obviously the Nordic States and the UK, but also perhaps France, which generally opposes stronger powers for the Parliament while supporting them for the Council. Anticipating this, the CDU/CSU authors also propose the repeal of Article N of the Treaty, under which unanimity among Member States is required for Treaty amendment (Schäuble and Lamers 1994, p. 16). This would open the way for basic decisions on the EU's constitution to be made by some (as yet unspecified) system of majority voting. Leading parliamentarians in Germany have thus given notice that a minority of States should not be allowed to block constitutional change in the Union. The document is not officially endorsed by the German government but it is probably broadly indicative of views among Germany's ruling centre-right parties.

It was not intended that the 1996 IGC should focus on EMU questions, but the conference could be important for EMU. There is nothing to stop EMU issues from being raised, and if worries about political economy aspects have crystallized since Maastricht, the IGC would be an appropriate opportunity to address them. Some governments have warned against reopening the EMU package, but that was before the referenda revealed widespread popular unease about the Treaty; circumstances have moved on since the short-lived period of post-Maastricht optimism, with convergence proving more difficult to secure than expected and second thoughts emerging about the details of Stage III. The possibility cannot be ruled out that if there is fundamental disagreement about political union, especially over steps which in German eyes are critical to the success of EMU, German support for an EMU on Maastricht lines might wane. This would cause the process to lose momentum, as Germany's participation in EMU has been seen as vital by other States, whereas many Germans continue to worry about the Bundesbank losing control over their currency. If EMU ran into problems, it might give way to lesser alternatives, such as a small D-mark bloc with a clear German hegemony. At present, such a development seems unlikely. The German government, and the political classes there generally, seem strongly attached to EMU as the clearest manifestation of the EC's ability to evolve into an economic and political union into which Germany could contentedly settle, submerging fears of a revival of past expansionism. After the recent French presidential election it has been possible to detect some attenuation of the Schäuble–Lamers message, suggesting that German political objectives will not be pushed in the IGC to the extent of jeopardizing EMU. If compromises are to be sought at the IGC in order to keep EMU on the road, a modest extension of the powers of the European Parliament in the monetary sphere, as suggested above, would have the dual appeal of strengthening the ECB's democratic accountability while promoting the German goal of wider consensus-building on EMU policy.

Implications for non-participants

A move to a small-group EMU around 1999 would pose hard choices for States which manage to achieve convergence by then but hesitate to join for political reasons. They could include Britain and some Nordic States.[4] Their decisions will depend in part on what are seen as the available alternatives. That will depend on which other EU States are outside EMU, i.e. those with a derogation, together with any that join the EU around the turn of the century. The more there are outside, whether through opt-out or derogation, the more likely it would be that special exchange-rate arrangements would be developed to accommodate them.

Apart from providing for the ECB *General* Council to take over the EMI's functions when Stage III starts, the Treaty is not specific about the arrangements for Member States outside EMU. The implicit assumption is that the ERM will continue in some form, for otherwise it would not be possible to continue applying the existing exchange-rate criterion, as the Treaty seems to envisage for States with a derogation wishing to join (*Treaty*, Article 109k.2). But the criterion could be redefined, and the ERM itself may evolve again in due course. Like the three latest, new Member States may not be required to join it. If the ERM or some successor arrangement continues, the EMU group would presumably form a currency bloc within it, and would dominate by size of output, trade and voting power in the Council (see Arrowsmith 1995, Tables 4 and 5). The 15% band might also continue, or be replaced or supplemented by narrower bands. Reforms might in due course be implemented in the system's operation, to make it more suitable for a post-EMU environment. The design of the system, as well as the thrust of policy within it, would presumably be determined largely by the EMU group as the dominant member, and this could well mean shifting more of the burden of intervention and associated costs onto the shoulders of borrowing countries, as well as more of the onus for policy correction.

Some non-EMU participants might choose to float outside the ERM or its successor, as several do now; others might prefer to peg unilaterally to the EMU bloc or informally shadow it, as several did in the past in relation to the ECU or the D-mark. Those that aspire to EMU will doubtless strive to maintain exchange-rate stability, *de facto* if not formally, against the EMU bloc, through determined monetary action when necessary. Their choice of arrangements will depend both on the Treaty criterion and their preferred focus for monetary policy (i.e. whether a domestic or external target).

At least initially after the start of Stage III, those outside are likely to suffer some penalty in the form of an increased interest-rate premium, but its size is hard to predict. If the markets believe that a country's exclusion is only a temporary setback and that firm policies will continue with a view to subsequent entry, the penalty might be small. But if a weakening of policy resolve is perceived the penalty could be sharp, reflecting both higher inflation expectations and greater uncertainty. In some cases, decisive policy action might be needed to reassure markets, which would probably mean a marked rise in short-term interest rates, although not necessarily long-term rates. Fears of permanent exclusion might lead to additional economic penalties, as illustrated by the British case below.

The choice for the UK

The United Kingdom is likely to face its crucial decision in autumn 1997. While an opt-out would not prejudice the UK's legal position under the Treaty or EU directives, it could appear very negative to other Member States and might provoke retaliation. In principle, Denmark would be in a similar situation unless it reverses its opt-out but, given the UK's size and influence in the Community, a British opt-out would doubtless be seen as more serious. Thus although the UK faces the basic economic calculus described in Chapters 5 and 6, there could be additional effects arising from an opt-out, bearing in mind also certain specific features of the UK economy, such as the importance of the financial sector and foreign investment in UK industry. To these factors should be added the major political-economy concerns discussed earlier – weak ECB accountability and possible conflict between monetary and fiscal policy leading to fiscal centralization. A full assessment of these factors would require a special study, beyond the scope of the present paper, but a number of points can be made in the light of the preceding discussion.

It should be borne in mind that the question here is purely about the effects of *EMU*; it does not cover those of the Single Market, to which Britain is assumed to belong regardless of its EMU decision. Although interrelated, these are separate issues, if often confused in popular discussion. It also helps to define the alternative UK policy case for purposes of comparison. This is assumed to be continuation of the status quo, in which sterling floats fairly freely – although it would make little economic difference if the pound were in an ERM with a 15% band. It is also assumed that UK monetary policy would continue to focus on an inflation target set by government and pursued by a Bank of England with some limited operational autonomy but not full legal independence.

Macroeconomic considerations
As compared with the status quo there would be, contrary to some views, a significant loss of monetary-policy sovereignty from joining EMU. Under managed floating, or an adjustable-peg regime with very wide bands like the present ERM, sterling would retain considerable flexibility against the EMU bloc. This would give quite wide scope for UK interest rates to differ from EMU rates, as now in relation to the ERM currencies. The scope would of course be limited by the wish to minimize exchange-rate instability, but external stability would not be a policy target.

As seen earlier, the desirability of retaining exchange-rate flexibility depends partly on how subject an economy is to asymmetric shocks. The UK has been more prone to such shocks than the core group, but the future is hard to read in this respect, both because the UK economy may converge further with the core and because the core may become more subject to asymmetries in time. The case for exchange-rate flexibility also depends on the UK's ability to run its own anti-inflation policy effectively. History is not reassuring here: the UK's inflation record in the past two decades has been distinctly less good than that of the core States, as Table 7.1 showed. However, public opinion seems to have become more seized of the benefits of price stability in recent years. The main reason for joining the ERM in 1990 was to lock the UK's already diminishing inflation rate into that of the ERM core; sterling's departure from the mechanism in 1992 was a serious defeat for that policy, and seen to be so. The policy arrangements introduced after that débâcle were important reforms which could mean a sea change in policy and attitudes.

Yet the efficacy of these new arrangements remains unsure for the time being. It depends heavily on the will and priorities of the government of the day, as well as on the personalities of the Chancellor and Bank Governor. However technically inclined the former may be to agree with the latter's judgment on the requirements of price stability, short-term political pressures may pull in other directions from time to time. Much also depends on the perceptions of wage bargainers and the financial markets. Inflation expectations will remain low provided they accept that price stability will have priority in the medium term, but such convictions are likely to be fragile, especially before general elections. The new policy approach has not yet been put to a severe test and in that case inflation uncertainties will persist, and the markets will demand a risk premium on sterling to reflect it. Estimates of that premium are hazardous, but recent experience suggests that joining EMU might mean lower real long-term interest rates for the UK by the order of $\frac{3}{4}$–1%, compared with the status quo. If maintained, this would provide a sizeable boost to investment in the longer run, recalling the arguments of Chapter 5.

Exchange-rate flexibility and monetary independence would also be desirable if the UK were to be, or become, uncompetitive externally for structural reasons. On this the evidence is moderately reassuring. As was seen in Chapter 7, UK competitiveness is unlikely to be a problem in the next few years, given sterling's depreciation, unless old inflationary habits re-emerge. But nagging doubts remain. The rather fragile improvement in the external current account noted in Chapter 7 recalls worries about the British chronic postwar trading weakness, masked by North Sea oil after the mid-1970s. On that view, a gradual long-run decline in sterling's real exchange rate is needed to offset erosion of international market share. There are signs recently that this trend has changed for the better, and the Single Market stimulus may bring further improvement relative to competitors both within and beyond Europe, but it is too early yet to be confident of this.

On these assessments, the fundamental economic case for this country's joining EMU seems tentatively favourable. Provided the UK economy has converged securely in real terms, and strong doubts remain about an independently run monetary policy, the macroeconomic arguments point on balance to joining: there would also be valuable long-term benefits through lower real interest rates, and modest savings in transactions costs when the single currency finally arrives.

Impact on industry

An opt-out might also affect British industry in ways not covered above. First, as noted, there might be acute resentment among governments and firms in the EMU group, and perhaps the EU more generally, at what could be seen as anti-European behaviour. Given that overt discrimination would be against Single Market law, this would (if it happened) mainly take the form of covert action against UK exports, investment, rights of establishment, public-sector procurement, etc., in ways which could be difficult to police but substantial in practice.[5] Secondly, an impression could develop of the UK as a 'second-tier' economy unable to compete on equal terms with the best in Europe. That would discourage investment in this country, particularly inward investment by international firms which have regarded the UK as an ideal bridgehead for trade with the Single Market. The major Japanese investments in electronics and motor vehicles of the past decade, which are now contributing strongly to the UK trade balance, are prime examples. Thirdly, an EMU opt-out could significantly disadvantage the UK financial sector, which has grown rapidly to become an important part of the economy (some 17% of GDP according to one recent study,[6] much larger than in most other EU economies), and which might be specially vulnerable to 'informal' discrimination, as will be explained below.

Any assessment of such effects is bound to be hazardous; much would depend on circumstances in particular cases. The fact that the UK would continue to be part of the Single Market despite an EMU opt-out means that discrimination would be subject to investigation by the competent authorities, and perhaps actionable before the European Court, and this would be an important safeguard. Moreover discrimination might not be widespread unless there were a clear perception that the UK was using its independence to exploit an unfair competitive advantage. This might be more likely in the case of social policy if the UK opt-out from the Community's social chapter is maintained. If an EMU opt-out ushered in an active UK policy of exchange-rate depreciation it would certainly be viewed as highly unfair in the Community, but it is assumed that this would not happen under the policy approach outside EMU, which would retain currency adjustment only as a last, market-driven, response to declining competitive power. In that case competitors might see little to merit retaliation. On the other hand, precisely for that reason, an opt-out against the background of non-accommodating monetary policy could reinforce an impression of UK industry as uncompetitive, and discourage inward investment.

Much would also depend on public and government attitudes in the UK, and on the way the country's position was presented. An expressly permanent opt-out would provoke a greater adverse reaction than a temporary, provisional, one. In fact, the UK will not be called upon to make a permanent decision, for a negative notification could be changed at any time after the beginning of Stage III (UK Protocol, Article 10). By indicating that it would review its position periodically, a UK government could hope to mitigate adverse international reactions. However, this would risk generating uncertainty, which would not help investment. And it might reduce UK influence on the planning of Stage III although, since the latter's main institutional and operational features should have been decided under the EMI's auspices before the UK decision is announced (given its effective postponement to 1997 or later), that might not matter much.

If a UK opt-out were carefully handled so as not to provoke European trading partners, and if by opting out freedom were retained to adjust sterling to maintain competitiveness while continuing to pursue non-inflationary monetary policies, inward investment would probably not be affected in a lasting way, except through enhanced uncertainty which might well persist for some years – and apart from the basic macroeconomic effects discussed earlier. Any additional effects of a UK opt-out on industrial investment generally might therefore be temporary, while industrialists assessed the new situation.

Impact on financial services

While this would apply broadly across industry, it might not do so in financial services. Foreign-currency business is an important activity in the financial sector, and many financial services are relatively mobile internationally, being characterized by low transport and communications costs, while tending to be reliant on interpersonal contact and trust, which makes them specially vulnerable to 'informal' protectionism.

However, even there generalization is difficult, because circumstances differ among different kinds of financial institution, e.g. between relatively short-term institutions like banks and securities houses, and long-term

142

institutions like insurance companies and pension funds. The case for special gains from EMU is strongest for the long-term funds, because international integration of capital markets would undoubtedly be boosted if exchange risk were eliminated; there would be much less need for pension funds and insurance companies to match their assets and liabilities in individual countries if there were a single currency or permanently fixed exchange rates. Because privately funded pension funds are substantially more prevalent in the UK than in continental economies, the British funds and their associated activities have more expertise in fund management than their European counterparts; and the demand for privately funded pensions seems bound to grow particularly fast on the continent as pay-as-you-go schemes impose increasing burdens on the public sector (Corby Report 1995). As the Single Market opens up, there should be attractive opportunities for UK fund managers and securities houses, which tend to have more experience of risk management because they operate in a more liberal domestic regulatory regime than their continental counterparts. EMU should help to exploit this competitive advantage, especially if and when Single Market directives eventually remove the remaining restrictions on insurance and pensions business and investments in continental centres.

The case for joining EMU is less strong, and perhaps negative, for short-term institutions; most clearly for firms specializing in foreign-exchange dealing, futures and options, which make their living from currency hedging and speculation (although intra-EC deals comprise less than 10% of the London foreign-exchange market). It is therefore not surprising that surveys of practitioner opinion among City institutions reveal a marked division of view, with only marginal balances in favour of EMU.[7] This is in contrast with surveys of industry, where opinion is usually more favourable to EMU, except among small businesses.

For major UK banks, the pros and cons seem fairly evenly balanced, especially when allowance is made for the special burden on them of converting to the single currency. Gains from economic integration in banking come not so much from working in domestic currency as from unrestricted access to large markets for similar services, in which economies of scale and scope can operate. The development of the Euro-currency markets in the past several decades testifies to this. Such gains depend much more on the harmonization of market conditions, specially regulatory systems and tax arrangements, than the elimination of currency differences. Especially in retail banking and other retail services, barriers to cross-border provision of services after a UK opt-out will matter less if UK firms can still branch across borders into EMU or set up subsidiaries there. There is, moreover, the possibility that any competitive disadvantage from covert discrimination against British firms would be offset by freedom from requirements imposed by the ECB for monetary-control purposes (such as unremunerated MRRs).

Savers in participating economies stand to gain significantly from the availability of a wider range of investment opportunities within EMU. Investment in continental equities and bonds will then be on a par with domestic investment in terms of exchange risk. However, the benefits for British savers are unlikely to be as great as for other EU savers, because UK intermediaries already offer a wide range of choice to their customers, including unrestricted opportunities to invest in foreign currency assets, whereas in most continental regimes portfolio choice is more restricted by prudential requirements which limit diversification. Moreover, gains from lower exchange risk could be offset by greater exposure to credit risk under EMU, if loss of exchange-rate flexibility means that the business environment becomes more difficult in some regions (e.g. through larger output cycles or adverse cost trends).

It is sometimes argued that financial business will be lost to London if the Bank of England does not participate in the ESCB, for the ECB would then concentrate its foreign-exchange and money-market operations in other centres. However, this effect on its own would not be large in relation to London's total business, partly because the ECB's own market operations will only be a small fraction of all business done in European centres, and partly because London is, and should remain, one of the world's largest and most efficient financial centres. Thus it would hardly be practicable for the ECB entirely to avoid routeing foreign-exchange transactions through the London market, or profitable for private banks in EMU to withdraw substantially from it. A more significant loss could eventually occur if major international banks relocate their European headquarters from London to Frankfurt when the ECB eventually starts operations there, as some may do if they believe that Britain will be permanently outside EMU. Such a move could be motivated by a wish to be close to the centres of market intelligence on a major global currency, assuming a single currency in EMU. However, the mere location of the ECB in Frankfurt would probably not in itself precipitate such an exodus, especially if ESCB operations were on a decentralized model. Only if Frankfurt threatened for other reasons to overtake London as the major European financial centre would a serious decampment of international banking business from London be likely. It is not easy to see an EMU opt-out as a prime cause of such a threat, although it might be a catalyst if other factors were to weaken London's competitive position.

The tentative conclusion here is that participation in EMU would probably be moderately beneficial for UK savers and City institutions as a whole in the long run. The main benefits would come from improvements in the 'fundamentals' – more price stability and less exchange risk – but there could be important offsets through greater credit risk in some regions, leaving the net effects relatively small and uncertain. The special effects of a UK opt-out would probably also not be major, mainly reflecting uncertainty and 'psychological' factors which, while they could be uncomfortable for a time, would probably not last unless the fundamentals changed.

Political economy

The ECB's weak accountability is at odds with British democratic traditions and with directions of reform proposed by the Treasury Select Committee and the Roll Committee. However, strengthening it would entail extending the powers of the other EU institutions – not something that is likely to appeal to the British electorate. Yet it would not be logical for supporters of the Maastricht model to resist enhancing the monetary powers of the European Parliament on national sovereignty grounds, since they will be ceded anyway to an ECB Governing Council over which national central-bank governors will exercise very limited individual influence. Resistance to such an enhancement is naturally to be expected from those who would oppose *any* strengthening of ECB accountability on the ground that it would weaken the institution's credibility, but their viewpoint assumes an absence of popular consensus on the price-stability objective. The wisdom of venturing upon EMU if such a consensus is absent would seem highly questionable.

Observers in this country who are broadly persuaded of the economic case for joining EMU may hesitate to recommend it because they fear that it will lead eventually to political centralization, on the ground that EMU will require a large central budget or a strong fiscal authority at Community level. This position overlooks the possibility that private investment flows will expand to meet some of the need for transfers under EMU. And it denies that adequate fiscal discipline would be exerted by market forces and peer-group pressure – a view which the UK Chancellor of the Exchequer himself expounded during the pre-Maastricht negotiations (Lamont 1991). It also denies that the 'excessive-deficit' procedure in the Treaty could be relied on to limit deficits. While worries about the efficacy of the Maastricht fiscal rules are understandable, it seems reasonable to expect that responsible governments committed to EMU would observe sensible fiscal rules. Fiscal irresponsibility within EMU cannot be totally ruled out, but participants would have the ultimate option of leaving EMU if they believed that key rules were not being observed. This feature of a Treaty-based EMU would distinguish it crucially from most existing monetary unions, whose constituent regions seldom have the option of secession, short of civil war.

Overall conclusion

For those who see EMU as a stepping stone to political integration in Europe, if not its cornerstone, the message from the above study is clear: the economic implications of EMU are not so unattractive to States which have converged securely that they should be deterred from using it to further their political objective. A single currency is certainly compatible with political integration, and perhaps essential to it, especially where common culture and language are lacking. Even so, EMU will not lead inexorably to political union. Pooling of sovereignty over monetary policy would be compatible with retention of much other economic power in national hands, and in a last resort it would be reversible, admittedly at some political cost.

For those who are not intent on European political integration, the case for EMU on its economic merits alone is much more open. Those who doubt the ability of their national authorities to pursue a successful monetary policy in the long run can reasonably see it as a persuasive alternative, but only if they are confident that their own economy and those of other candidates have converged closely in real as well as nominal terms, and are not subject to major structural weaknesses; and they must also be confident that public opinion will accept and respond cooperatively to the low-inflation environment of EMU. In those circumstances, the gains from price stability, lower real interest rates through the elimination of exchange-rate uncertainty, and savings in currency-conversion costs are eminently worth securing, whereas monetary sovereignty is not worth retaining. Furthermore, the economic status quo might not be totally unaffected if the movement towards EMU were aborted now. For example, some rationalization of industrial and financial operations might have to be undone if abandonment of EMU triggered changes in policy priorities, as Panic (1992) has pointed out.

Those who, in contrast, have faith in their national authorities to run monetary policy successfully face a more difficult choice, for then there could be genuine advantages in retaining monetary sovereignty outside EMU, even at the cost of living with more exchange-rate certainty and higher transactions costs. In this respect, the country which has least to gain and most to lose economically from pooling monetary sovereignty is undoubtedly Germany. Without strong political objectives it would be hard to see why Germany should be interested in joining EMU, beyond gaining the modest benefits that currency stability with its main trading partners would bring.

For the UK the choice, abstracting from purely political objectives, is still a close one. The message in this study is that the economic arguments marginally favour joining an EMU on Maastricht lines, subject to several important provisos. First, in addition to nominal inflation convergence, real convergence, particularly of UK cost levels, must be securely estab- lished before joining. There seems a reasonable prospect of this in the next few years, but only if inflation remains subdued and the UK's postwar weakness in trade performance has been genuinely overcome. Secondly, changes should be made in the Treaty to strengthen the ECB's accountability, on lines indicated in Chapter 8. Thirdly, modifications should be made in the fiscal rules to increase their flexibility, add an element of policy coordination and make the sanctions more predictable, as also outlined there. These fiscal modifications could be made by political decision in the Council, and would not require Treaty amendment.

The UK should be prepared to opt into an EMU of perhaps six to eight countries at the end of the century if and when the government and parliament of the day are satisified that convergence has been securely established and if appropriate institutional modifications can be agreed. If it has doubts about convergence, including convergence of real factors, whether at home or among other candidates, the UK should remain outside until they are removed by better economic performance, while explaining its reservations to EU colleagues. In the meantime, it should be prepared to hold out, in a constructive way, for improvements in the Maastricht blueprint of the kind outlined. Given that there are strong political and economic reasons for both France and Germany to want the UK to join EMU, modest improvements in the institutional design should not be out of reach. They should strike a sympathetic chord among nations which prize democracy as well as stability, and other EU States should not take offence at this country seeking them, provided it is done in a positive spirit that looks forward to EMU membership in due course.

Notes

Chapter 2: The Maastricht Treaty

1 The Treaty was signed on 7 February 1992.
2 Here and later, references to *Statute* are to the Statute of the ESCB and ECB.
3 Here and later, references to *Treaty* are to the Treaty on European Union.
4 This procedure is already in operation in Stage II, as is the excessive-deficits procedure.
5 An account of the EMI and its role can be found in Bank of England (1994).
6 The decision on fixing will be by *unanimity* of participating States, which could enable individual States to veto or delay the start, a point which has not been lost on the German authorities. In theory, it would be possible to choose a markedly different set of conversion rates and still leave the ECU's external value unchanged, but this could create problems – see Chapter 7, note 4.
7 Indeed the Treaty does not say that eligibility requires meeting all or any of the criteria, as Kenen (1995b) has pointed out. Their purpose is 'to guide the Community in taking decisions' ('Protocol on the convergence criteria', preamble).

Chapter 3: The road to Maastricht

1 Graboyes (1990) gives an account of the LMU's operation and fate. See also Dyson (1994), pp. 25–9. A full history and analysis of developments leading to EMU can be found in Part 1 of Dyson (ibid.).
2 An analysis of the operation of the classical gold standard and lessons for EMU can be found in Panic (1992). See also Eichengreen (1985) and Dyson (1994).
3 Britain had been on a full legal gold standard since 1821; Germany adopted it after 1871, and the United States in 1879.

4 To a limited extent, a rationale for fixed exchange rates did exist in the form of French concern about the problems posed by variable exchange rates for the Common Agricultural Policy (which aims at uniform agricultural prices across the Community), and the customs union generally; this was to be a recurrent theme in later planning for monetary integration (Dyson 1994, chapter 3).

5 A description of its main operational features can be found in Bank of England (1990) and a review of the research literature in Bank of England (1991). See also Ungerer et al., 1990 and Gros and Thygesen (1992).

6 For a defence of the report by one of its independent authors, see Thygesen (1989). An economic critique can be found in Kenen (1991).

7 The Report nevertheless advised against setting rigid deadlines (Committee for the Study of Economic and Monetary Union 1989, p. 32), contrary to what the Treaty provided.

Chapter 4: Is the EC an optimal currency area?

1 Correspondence with the author, May 1995.

2 The seminal articles are Barro and Gordon (1983) and Barro (1985).

3 The reasoning here is not that asymmetric shocks are more damaging than symmetric ones, but that asymmetric shocks demand different policy responses, which may be difficult in EMU.

Chapter 5: One market, one money

1 A review can be found in International Monetary Fund (1984). See also Bank of England (1984).

2 Furthermore, financial instruments cannot be used to hedge against exchange-rate risk when exchange-rate changes affect levels of production or sales, because the amounts to be hedged are then uncertain, as Kenen (1995a, p. 180) notes.

3 British Bankers' Association (1993), the Association for the Monetary Union of Europe (1994) and the Banking Federation of the European Union (1995).

4 The corresponding period needed for UK decimalization, a much simpler exercise, was over five years.

5 The multipliers are calculated from Baldwin's estimated aggregate production functions in the main EC economies and attempt to capture the combined effects on output of a once-for-all upward shift in the production function and the increase in the capital stock induced by the associated increase in the marginal productivity of capital, using a standard neoclassical growth-theory approach (Baldwin 1991). While growth multipliers of this magnitude are not implausible, the estimates are subject to a wide margin of error, as illustrated by the results for individual States, which

range from a low of 1.24 for the United Kingdom to a high of 2.4 for Belgium (Commission 1990, Table 3.9). It seems unlikely that the properties of production functions could actually differ by so much between those relatively compatible economies.

6 Not all the GDP increase would represent a welfare gain; some would comprise increased investment (Thygesen 1993).

7 A recent review of the theoretical arguments and empirical evidence can be found in Briault (1995).

Chapter 6: Adjusting without the exchange rate

1 This is consistent with Kenen's early stress on product diversification, and the recent empirical work by Bini-Smaghi and Vori (1992) on US/EC production patterns, discussed in Chapter 4.

2 Seigniorage from the note issue and unremunerated deposits at national central banks will not disappear under EMU. It will continue to be received by ESCB central banks and distributed to their governments, but it is expected to shrink from present levels because inflation, and banks' minimum reserve ratios, will mostly be lower, especially in less developed States (see Commission 1993a, pp. 89–90).

3 A further reservation is that the scheme involves general intergovernment transfers, not direct payments to the unemployed, so that governments may use them merely to reduce their deficits (Kenen, in correspondence with the author, May 1995).

Chapter 7: The transition

1 Some of these objections could equally be levelled at the single currency of Stage III.

2 Although the protocol is not precise, it is generally assumed that the standard is the (unweighted) *average* of inflation in the three States with the lowest inflation rates, not the third-lowest inflation rate, which could be significantly higher.

3 Bishop (1995, p.13) also points out that the reference to the bond yields of the 'three best-performing member states in terms of price stability' could create anomalies, in that Commission forecasts suggest that the best performers in 1996 will be Finland, France and the Netherlands, whose bond rates all exceed equivalent German bond rates.

4 This is of course the essence of the case for 'one last realignment', but a substantial realignment after the decision to start Stage III could be hard to achieve if it meant devaluation of the D-mark, especially given the Treaty requirement that the ECU's external value be kept unchanged.

5 At present, Germany as a high-cost producer (reflecting the strong D-

mark) can regain competitiveness by inflating more slowly than its partners. But assuming the latter approach price stability under EMU, Germany would have to disinflate to regain competitiveness.

6 As usual, the forecasts are based on the technical assumption of unchanged nominal exchange-rates for ERM currencies and fixed real rates for non-ERM currencies, taking as starting point the average of rates in March 1995. They therefore exclude the effects of currency changes since then.

7 US dollars in Turner and Van't dack's original calculations, but for relative costs the currency does not matter.

8 The fall of measured unemployment in Portugal may reflect the exceptionally rapid economic growth there in the 1980s, stemming partly from inward investment, together with a sizeable self-employed farming and small business sector.

9 This assumes some limited reinterpretation of the exchange-rate criterion by the Council: the 12 Member States which agreed the Maastricht Treaty will be required to have been formal members of the ERM from 1 January 1995, without initiating a devaluation, and to have remained comfortably within the 15% band. The new Member States will be required to have maintained a similar degree of stability against the ERM core currencies, but not necessarily to have formally joined.

10 Countries which opt out will not count towards a majority. However, it is assumed here that they will continue to be included in the *denominator* of the majority ratio, although the Treaty is not explicit on that point.

11 If the Council decides that a 12-month period of preparation is needed between the key decisions and the start of Stage III in January 1999, as looks increasingly likely, the second assessment will have to be made by end-1997.

12 The EMI is already letting it be known publicly that it is seriously concerned about fiscal developments in Member States. There are repeated statements to this effect in its first annual report, where it also notes that it expressed its concern about the state of public finances to the Council on two occasions in the spring of 1994 (European Monetary Institute 1995).

13 This will not mean giving the ECU equal status with domestic currencies in Stage II; there is no intention, for example, to give the ECU legal tender status. Rather, the aim is to give it equivalent status to other foreign currencies, which it presently lacks in some Member States, notably Germany and the UK.

14 It is sometimes suggested that the existing ECU clearing system could be the embryo for the single currency's clearing system in Stage III. However, this reflects a misunderstanding of what Stage III will involve – namely the linking together of existing clearing systems for *national* currencies.

15 Some senior German politicians and bankers are reported still to believe that 'ecu' will not be acceptable as the name of the single currency there.

The first published text of the Maastricht Treaty used 'ecu' throughout, but on German insistence all references had to be changed to 'ECU', signifying the European Currency Unit, a more neutral term.

Chapter 8: The anatomy of Stage III

1 Some commentators argue that this provision means that the ECB will be obliged to issue ECU in monetary form from day one, but that seems to go beyond the intentions of the rest of Article 109l.4. Article 52 of the ESCB Statute says that national central banks must exchange national banknotes at par after the locking of rates, but says nothing about exchanging them for ECU. However, if the ECU's exchange-rate against national currencies is to be irrevocably fixed, ESCB central banks will presumably have to be prepared to buy and sell ECU at that rate, which could entail issuing new ECU to the market.

2 This implies some further integration of national payments systems at wholesale level, to give banks the ability to make cross-border transfers of interbank positions and achieve final same-day settlement.

3 Commercial banks could continue to operate in existing currencies, except that they would hold some of their operating balances in ECU with the ESCB, and trade them on the ECB Funds market.

4 A somewhat similar sequence has been suggested by the Maas Group, although it may be doubted whether the whole process could be completed within the six months envisaged by that Group (Expert Group on the Changeover to the Single Currency [Maas Group], *The Preparation of the Changeover to the Single European Currency*, Interim Report, submitted to the European Commission, 20 January 1995). The Commission's Green Paper on the introduction of the single currency (Commission 1995b), which came too late for full consideration here, suggests three years between the start of Stage III and the final switch to the single currency, but this too seems on the optimistic side.

5 There would be some parallel here with present British practice, for UK Select Committees do not press governors to reveal their confidential discussions with the Chancellor of the Exchequer. But governors cannot refuse to give a Select Committee their views on monetary policy without risking being found in contempt of Parliament.

6 For a fuller discussion, see Swinburne and Castello-Branco 1991, especially pp. 15–20 and Part IV. Guitian observes that adoption of a government override will not necessarily weaken the long-term thrust of an independent monetary policy, provided it is transparent and subject to parliamentary confirmation. The latter features mean that government itself is accountable for any interruption in policy. Such arrangements may make it possible to avoid damaging confrontations between government and

central bank, and make policy less susceptible to covert pressures, and to the particular personalities of finance minister and central-bank governor. The temporary nature of the override means that disagreements centre not on the long-term thrust of policy, but on short-term trade-offs between inflation and employment or internal/external currency stability objectives.

7 The Roll Committee also recommended the introduction of statutory backing for cash ratio deposits at the Bank of England, which would incidentally facilitate long-term accountability to Parliament through its influence over the Bank's finances.

8 ERM-type arrangements might continue with non-participating States after the start of Stage III, but provided they did not oblige the ECB to adjust its policies or intervene without limit to support their currencies, its price stability objective need not be prejudiced.

9 Italy accounts at present for about 40% of total EC public debt, and the proportion is unlikely to fall much.

10 There is no provision for payments under the structural funds to be suspended under this procedure.

11 All Member States are covered by the excessive-deficits procedure, although only participants in EMU will be liable to sanctions; it would therefore be possible to include all in the combined fiscal target. Whether it would make sense to do so would depend on how far non-participants in EMU shared the general thrust of its monetary policies.

12 See Monticelli and Viñals (1993) for a review of the issues.

13 Cassard et al. (1994, p. 20) point out that the properties of the equations look odd in several respects. See also Sardelis (1993) for a review of the empirical research and associated issues.

14 The basis of those reserves (e.g. the categories of assets or liabilities to which they relate), and maximum permissible ratios, will, however, be set by ECOFIN).

15 Harmonization of MRRs, as of other operational instruments, is not necessary for the conduct of a single monetary policy by the ESCB, because interest-rate arbitrage would in any case lead to a single monetary stance throughout EMU (Monticelli and Viñals 1993, p. 15). However, absence of harmonization could lead to relocation of financial activity which would probably be inefficient and which could distort the policy signals given to markets (ibid.).

16 Reserves at the central bank in excess of the 'required' level would not be remunerated.

17 For a fuller discussion, see Monticelli and Viñals (1993), section 4.

18 This suggests that MRRs and standing facilities may feature prominently in the early years of Stage III, but recede in importance later on (Viñals 1994, p. 34).

Chapter 9: The decisions ahead

1 It is sometimes argued, even by British Members of Parliament, that accountability for monetary policy is weak in Britain, because there is little formal opportunity to influence policy through debates on the floor of the House of Commons. They miss the point that the government's authority over policy depends on its ability to command continuing majority support in the Commons, which is in turn sensitive to public opinion. No one who witnessed the UK government's reluctance to raise interest rates in the summer of 1992, despite looming pressures on sterling, should doubt that monetary policy in this country can be highly subject to popular influence at times.

2 Only MEPs from States participating in EMU would be permitted to vote on questions relating to the policies and functions of the ECB.

3 There is clearly an analogy here with the multi-speed process under which countries will join EMU, as Schäuble and Lamers point out.

4 All the Nordic States will require further referenda before joining Stage III.

5 There is wording in Single Market directives to the effect that retaliatory measures could be justified if a Member State pursues unfair competitive policies. But an EMU opt-out under provisions agreed in the Treaty would, in itself, hardly qualify for such retaliatory treatment.

6 See London Business School/Corporation of London (1995), Figure 2-2.

7 For example, a Harris survey of senior managers in 250 City institutions conducted in December 1994 reported that 38% of respondents believed that EMU would increase business opportunities for the City, 32% believed that it would mean a decrease, 25% foresaw no effect and 5% were not sure. See London Securities and Derivatives Exchange (OMLX) (1994).

References

Alesina, A. (1989), 'Politics and Business Cycles in Industrial Democracies', *Economic Policy*, 8.

Alesina, A. and L. Summers (1988), 'Central Bank Independence and Macroeconomic Performance: Some Comparative Evidence', *Journal of Money, Credit and Banking*, 25, May.

Alogoskoufis, G. and R. Portes (1991), 'International Costs and Benefits from EMU', in Commission of the EC, 'The Economics of EMU', *European Economy*, Special Edition, 1.

Arrowsmith, J. (1995), 'Economic and Monetary Union in a Multi-Tier Europe', *National Institute Economic Review*, May.

Artis, M. J. (1994), *Stage Two: Feasible Transitions to EMU*, London: Centre for Economic Policy Research, Discussion Pape 928, March.

Association for the Monetary Union of Europe (1994), *Preparing the Transition to the Single Currency*, report by an AMUE working group chaired by M. Levitt, May.

Baer, G.D. and T. Padoa-Schioppa (1989), 'The Werner Report Revisited', in Committee for the Study of Economic and Monetary Union (Delors Committee) *Report on Economic and Monetary Union in the European Community*.

Baldwin, R. E. (1991), 'On the Microeconomics of the European Monetary Union', in Commission of the EC, 'The Economics of EMU', *European Economy*, Special Edition, 1.

Bank for International Settlements (1994), *64th Annual Report*, Basle, June.

Banking Federation of the European Union (1995), *Survey on the Introduction of the Single Currency: A First Contribution on the Practical Aspects*, FBE, March.

Bank of England (1972), *Quarterly Bulletin,* March.

Bank of England (1984), 'The Variability of Exchange Rates: Measurement and Effects', *Quarterly Bulletin*, September.

155

References

Bank of England (1990), *Quarterly Bulletin*, November.

Bank of England (1991), *Quarterly Bulletin*, February.

Bank of England (1994), 'The Role of the European Monetary Institute', *Quarterly Bulletin*, February.

Banque de France (1993), *Loi No. 93–980 du 4 août 1993 relative au Statut de la Banque de France et à l'activité et au contrôle des établissements de crédit*, Banque de France Bulletin Trimestriel, 88, December.

Barr, D. (1992), 'The Demand for Money in Europe: Comment on Kremers and Lane', IMF *Staff Papers,* 39, September.

Barrell, R. and J. Whitley (1992), 'Introduction' to Barrell and Whitley, eds, *Macroeconomic Policy Coordination in Europe: The ERM and Monetary Union*, London: Sage Publications for the National Institute of Economic and Social Research.

Barro, R.J. (1985) 'Recent Developments in the Theory of Rules versus Discretion', *Economic Journal*, 95, Supplement.

Barro, R.J. and D. Gordon (1983), 'A Positive Theory of Monetary Policy in a Natural Rate Model', *Journal of Political Economy*, 91 (4).

Bayoumi, T. and B. Eichengreen (1992), *Shocking Aspects of European Monetary Integration*, London: Centre for Economic Policy Research, Discussion Paper 643.

Bayoumi, T. and P.R. Masson (1991), 'Fiscal Flaws in the United States and Canada: Lessons for Monetary Union in Europe', International Monetary Fund working paper.

Begg, D. (1991), 'Alternative Exchange-rate Regimes: the Role of the Exchange Rate and the Implications for Wage–Price Adjustment', in Commission of the EC, 'The Economics of EMU', *European Economy*, Special Edition, 1.

Begg, D., Giavazzi, F., Spaventa, L. and C. Wyplosz (1991), 'European Monetary Union – the Macro Issues', in *Monitoring European Integration: The Making of Monetary Union*, London: Centre for Economic Policy Research.

Begg, I. and D. Mayes (1992), 'Cohesion as a Precondition for Monetary Union in Europe', in Ray Barrel, ed., *Economic Convergence and Monetary Union in Europe*, London: Sage Publications for the Association for the Monetary Union of Europe and the National Institute of Economic and Social Research.

Begg, I. and D. Mayes (1993), 'Cohesion in the European Community: Key Imperatives for the 1990's?', *Regional Science and Urban Economics*, 23.

Bini-Smaghi, L. and S. Vori (1992), 'Rating the EC as an Optimal Currency Area', in R. O'Brien, ed., *Finance and the International Economy*, 6, Oxford: Oxford University Press for the Amex Bank Review.

Bishop, G. (1991a), *Eculand – the Thirteenth Member of the EC*, Salomon Brothers Inc., April.

156

Bishop, G. (1991b), *Valuing Public Debt in the EC: EMU versus 'No-Bail-Out' Risks*, Salomon Brothers Inc., November.

Bishop, G. (1991c), *The Draft EMU Treaty: Key Questions Remain*, Salomon Brothers Inc., November.

Bishop, G. (1995). *The Single Currency: The European Commission's Green Paper*, Salomon Brothers Inc., June.

Bishop, G., Damrau, D. and M. Miller (1989), *Market Discipline CAN work in the EC Monetary Union*, Salomon Brothers Inc., November.

Bliss, C. (1994). *Economic Theory and Trade Blocs*, Manchester University Press.

Bofinger, P. (1994), 'Is Europe an Optimum Currency Area?', in A. Steinherr, ed., *30 Years of European Monetary Integration: From the Werner Plan to EMU*, London: Longman.

Briault, C. (1995), 'The Costs of Inflation', *Bank of England Quarterly Bulletin*, February.

British Bankers' Association (1993), *Implementation of a Single European Currency: Report on a Survey of UK Banks and Building Societies*, BBA/APACS, February.

Bruno, M. and J. Sachs (1985), *Economics of Worldwide Stagflation*, Cambridge, Mass.: National Bureau of Economic Research.

Buiter, W., Corsetti, G. and N. Roubini (1993), 'Excessive Deficits: Sense and Nonsense in the Treaty of Maastricht', *Economic Policy*, April.

Cassard, M., Lane, T. and P.R. Masson (1994), *ERM Money Supplies and the Transition to EMU*, IMF Working Paper, January.

Cohen, D. and C. Wyplosz (1989), *The European Monetary Union: An Agnostic Evaluation*, London: Centre for Economic Policy Research, Discussion Paper 306, April.

Commission of the European Communities (1988), 'The Economics of 1992' (The Cecchini Report), *European Economy*, 35, March.

Commission of the European Communities (1990), 'One Market, One Money', *European Economy*, 44, October.

Commission of the European Communities (1991), 'The Economics of EMU', *European Economy*, Special Edition, 1.

Commission of the European Communities (1993a), 'Stable Money – Sound Finances', *European Economy*, 53.

Commission of the European Communities (1993b), 'Annual Economic Report for 1993', *European Economy*, 54.

Commission of the European Communities (1994), 'Recent Economic Trends', *European Economy*, Supplement A, May.

Commission of the European Communities (1995a), 'Recent Economic Trends, *European Economy*, Supplement A, May.

Commission of the European Communities (1995b), *Green Paper on the Practical Arrangements for the Introduction of the Single Currency*, June.

157

References

Committee for the Study of Economic and Monetary Union (Delors Committee) (1989), *Report on Economic and Monetary Union in the European Community*, Luxembourg.

Corby Report (1995), *The Pension Time Bomb in Europe*, Rapporteur: Dick Taverne, Report of a study group chaired by Sir B. Corby, London: The Federal Trust for Education and Research.

Corden, W. M. (1972), *Monetary Integration*, Essays in International Finance, 93, Princeton, New Jersey.

Corden, W. M. (1993), 'European Monetary Union: The Intellectual Pre-History', in A. Giovannini, M. Guitian and R. Portes, eds, *The Monetary Future of Europe*, London: Centre for Economic Policy Research Discussion Paper, March.

Council of the European Communities/Commission of the European Communities (1992), *Treaty on European Union*, Luxembourg.

Crockett, A. D. (1994), 'The Role of Convergence in the Process of EMU', in A. Steinherr, ed., *30 Years of European Monetary Integration: From the Werner Plan to EMU*, London: Longman.

Cukierman, A. (1983), 'Relative Price Variability and Inflation: A Survey and Further Results', *Carnegie–Rochester Series on Public Policy,* 19.

Cukierman, A., Kalaitzidakis, P., Summers, L. and S. Webb (1993), 'Central Bank Independence, Growth, Investment and Real Rates', *Carnegie–Rochester Series on Public Policy*, 39, December.

Cukierman, A., Webb, S. and B. Neypati (1992), 'Measuring the Independence of Central Banks and its Effect on Policy Outcomes', *World Bank Economic Review*, September.

Currie, D. (1992), 'European Monetary Union: Institutional Structure and Economic Performance', *Economic Journal*, March.

De Grauwe, P. (1992), *The Economics of Monetary Integration*, Oxford: Oxford University Press.

De Grauwe, P. (1994), 'Towards European Monetary Union without the EMS', *Economic Policy*, 18.

Deutsche Bundesbank (1993), 'Ideas concerning a Monetary Strategy for Europe', in *Deutsche Bundesbank Annual Report 1992*.

Dornbusch, R. (1990), 'Two-Track EMU, Now!', in K.-O. Pöhl et al., *Britain and EMU*, London: Centre for Economic Performance, London School of Economics and Political Science, November.

Dowd, K. and D. Greenaway (1993), 'Currency Competition, Network Externalities and Switching Costs: Towards an Alternative View of Optimal Currency Areas', *Economic Journal*, September.

Dunnett, D. R. R. (1994), 'Legal and Institutional Issues affecting Monetary Union', in D. O'Keefe and P. M. Twomey, eds, *Legal Issues of the Maastricht Treaty*, Chichester: Chancery Law Publishing.

Dyson, K. (1994), *Elusive Union: The Progress of Economic and Monetary*

Union in Europe, London: Longman.

Easton, W. W. and M. J. Stephenson (1990), 'The Interest Rate Transmission Mechanism in the United Kingdom and Overseas', *Bank of England Quarterly Bulletin*, May.

Eichengreen, B. (ed.) (1985), *The Gold Standard in Theory and History*, London: Methuen.

Eichengreen, B. (1990a) 'One Money for Europe? Lessons from the U.S. Currency Union', *Economic Policy*, 10, April.

Eichengreen, B. (1990b), *Is Europe an Optimal Currency Area?*, London: Centre for Economic Policy Research, Discussion Paper 478, November.

Eichengreen, B. and C. Wyplosz (1993), 'The Unstable EMS', *Brookings Papers on Economic Activity*, 1.

Eijffinger, S. and E. Schaling (1993), *Central Bank Independence: Theory and Evidence*, Center for Economic Research, Tilburg University, Discussion Paper 9325, April.

European Monetary Institute (1995), *Annual Report 1994*, Frankfurt am Main, April.

Fischer, S. (1993), 'The Role of Macroeconomic Factors in Growth', *Journal of Monetary Economics*, December.

Fischer, S. (1994), *Modern Central Banking*, paper prepared for the Tercentenary of the Bank of England, Central Banking Symposium, 9 June.

Giavazzi F. and M. Pagano (1988), 'The Advantage of Tying One's Hands: EMS Discipline and Central Bank Credibility', *European Economic Review*, No 32.

Giavazzi, F. and L. Spaventa (1990), 'The New EMS', in P. De Grauwe and L. Papademos, eds, *The European Monetary System in the 1990's*, London: Longman.

Giovannini, A. (1990), 'European Monetary Reform: Progress and Prospects', *Brookings Papers on Economic Activity*, 2.

Giovannini, A. (1993), 'Central Banking in a Monetary Union: Reflections on the Proposed Statute of the European Central Bank', *Carnegie–Rochester Series on Public Policy*, 38.

Goodhart, C. A. E. (1992a), 'The ESCB after Maastricht', in Goodhart, ed., *EMU and the ESCB after Maastricht*, London: Financial Markets Group, London School of Economics and Political Science.

Goodhart, C. A. E. (1992b), 'The External Dimensions of EMU', in Goodhart, ed., *EMU and ESCB after Maastricht*, London: Financial Markets Group, London School of Economics and Political Science.

Goodhart, C. A. E. (1993), *The Political Economy of Monetary Union*, draft in mimeo, March. Reprinted in P. B. Kenen, ed., *Understanding Interdependence: The Macroeconomics of the Open Economy*, Princeton: Princeton University Press (forthcoming 1995).

Goodhart, C. and S. Smith (1993), 'Stabilization', in Commission of the EC,

References

'The Economics of Community Public Finance', *European Economy: Reports and Studies*, 5.

Graboyes, R. F. (1990), 'The EMU: Forerunners and Durability', *Federal Reserve Bank of Richmond Economic Review*, July/August.

Grice, J. (1990), 'The UK Proposals for a European Monetary Fund and a "Hard ECU": Making Progress Towards a Monetary Union in Europe', *HM Treasury Bulletin*, October.

Grilli, V., Masciandaro, D. and G. Tabellini (1991), 'Political and Monetary Institutions and Public Financial Policies in the Industrial Countries', *Economic Policy*, 13, October.

Gros, D. and N. Thygesen (1992), *European Monetary Integration: From the European Monetary System to European Monetary Union*, Longman: London.

Guitian, M. (1995), *Central Bank Independence: Issues and Diversity of Models*, paper prepared for a workshop on 'Independence and Accountability: The Role and Structure of the South African Reserve Bank', organized by the CEPR and the Centre for Research into Economics and Finance in South Africa, Pretoria, 9–10 January.

International Monetary Fund (1984), *Exchange-rate Variability and World Trade*, Occasional Paper, 28.

Issing, O. (1992), 'Theoretical and Empirical Foundations of the Deutsche Bundesbank's Monetary Targeting', *Intereconomics*, November-December.

Issing, O. (1994), 'Monetary Policy Strategy in the EMU', in J.O. de Beaufort Wijnholds, S. Eiffinger and L.H. Hoogduin, eds, *A Framework for Monetary Stability*, Amsterdam: Kluwer Academic Publishers.

Italianer, A. and M. Vanheukelen (1993), 'Proposals for Community Stabilization Mechanisms: Some Historical Applications', in Commission of the EC, 'The Economics of Community Public Finance', *European Economy*, Reports and Studies, 5.

Jenkins, R. (1977), 'Europe's Present Challenge and Future Opportunity', *First Jean Monnet Lecture*, Florence: European University Institute, 27 October.

Johnson, C. (1994), *The New Wide-band Exchange-rate Mechanism: Rules versus Discretion in a Target Zone*, International Monetary Fund Seminar Paper, mimeo, July.

Kenen, P. B. (1969), 'The Theory of Optimal Currency Areas: An Eclectic View', *Monetary Problems of the International Economy*, University of Chichago Press.

Kenen, P. B. (1991), 'From EMS to EMU and Beyond', *The Bosman Lecture*, Tilburg: Tilburg University, 10 April.

Kenen, P. B. (1992), *EMU After Maastricht*, Washington, DC: Group of Thirty.

Kenen, P. B. (1995a), *Economic and Monetary Union in Europe: Moving Beyond Maastricht*, Cambridge and New York: Cambridge University Press (forthcoming).

Kenen, P. B. (1995b), *Hazards on the Road to the Third Stage of Economic and Monetary Union*, paper for the Forum for US–EC Legal-Economic Affairs Session on Issues of Governance in the European Community. London, September 1995, draft in mimeo.

Kremers, J. M. and T. D. Lane (1990), 'Economic and Monetary Integration and the Aggregate Demand for Money in the EMS', IMF *Staff Papers*, 37, December.

Krugman, P. R. (1990), 'Policy Problems of a Monetary Union', reprinted in Krugman, ed., *Currencies and Crises*, Cambridge, Mass.: MIT Press, 1992.

Krugman, P. R. (1992), 'Integration, Specialisation, and Regional Growth: Notes on 1992, EMU and Stabilization', paper presented at the International Conference 'The Transition to Economic and Monetary Union in Europe', Banco de Portugal and CEPR, January.

Lamont, N. (1991), 'British Objectives for Monetary Union in Europe', Speech to an AMUE/RIIA Conference 'European Monetary Union in a Turbulent World Economy', May. Reprinted in *De Pecunia*, Association for the Monetary Union of Europe, June.

London Business School/Corporation of London (1995), *The Competitive Position of London's Financial Services: Final Report of the City Research Project*, London: Corporation of London, March.

London Securities and Derivatives Exchange (OMLX) (1994), *EMU City Survey*, December.

Maas Group (1995), *The Preparation of the Changeover to the Single European Currency*, Interim Report of the Expert Group on the Changeover to the Single Currency, submitted to the European Commission, January.

MacDougall Report (1977), *Report of the Study Group on the Role of Public Finance in European Integration*, Commission of the EC.

Masson, P. R. and J. Melitz (1990), *Fiscal Policy Independence in a European Monetary Union*, London: Centre for Economic Policy Research Discussion Paper, 414, April.

Masson, P. R. and S. Symansky (1992), 'Evaluating the EMS and EMU using Stochastic Simualations: Some Issues', in R. Barrel and J. Whitley, eds, *Macroeconomic Policy Coordination in Europe: The ERM and Monetary Union*, London: Sage Publications for the National Institute of Economic and Social Research.

McKinnon, R. I. (1963), 'Optimal Currency Areas', *American Economic Review*, 53 (4), September.

Meade, J. and M. Weale (1992), *On the Stability of Monetary and Fiscal Policy*, Department of Applied Economics, University of Cambridge Discussion Paper, revised January.

Melliss, C. L. and M. Cornelius (1994), 'New Currencies in the Former Soviet Union: A Recipe for Hyperinflation or the Path to Price Stability?', *Bank of England Working Paper Series*, 26, September.

References

Minford, P., Rastogi, A. and A. Hughes-Hallet (1992), 'ERM and EMU –
    Survival, Costs and Prospects', in R. Barrell and J. Whitley, eds,
    *Macroeconomic Policy Coordination in Europe: The ERM and Monetary
    Union*, London: Sage Publications for the National Institute of Economic
    and Social Research.

Monticelli, C. and M.-O. Strauss-Kahn (1993), 'European Integration and the
    Demand for Broad Money', *Manchester School of Economics and Social
    Studies*, LXI, 4, December.

Monticelli, C. and J. Viñals (1993), 'European Monetary Policy in Stage
    Three: What are the Issues?', in A. Giovannini et al., eds, *The Monetary
    Future of Europe*, London: Centre for Economic Policy Research, March.

Mundell, R. A. (1961), 'A Theory of Optimal Currency Areas', *American
    Economic Review*, 60 (4), September.

Mundell, R. A. (1963), 'Capital Mobility and Stabilization Policy under Fixed
    and Flexible Exchange Rates', *Canadian Journal of Economics and
    Political Science*, 29, November.

Neumann, M. J. M. (1991), 'Central Bank Independence as a Prerequisite of
    Price Stability', in Commission of the EC, 'The Economics of EMU',
    European Economy, Special Edition, 1.

Neumann, M. J. M. and J. von Hagen (1991), 'Conditional Relative Price
    Variance and its Determinants: Open Economy Evidence from Germany',
    International Economic Review, February.

OECD (1986), *Flexibility in the Labour Market*, Paris.

Panic, M. (1992), *European Monetary Union: Lessons from the Classical Gold
    Standard*, London: St Martin's Press.

Papadia, F. and F. Saccomanni (1994), 'From the Werner Plan to the
    Maastricht Treaty: Europe's Stubborn Quest for Monetary Union', in A.
    Steinherr, ed., *30 Years of European Monetary Integration: From the
    Werner Plan to EMU*, London: Longman.

Pisani-Ferry, J., Italianer, A. and R. Lescure (1993), 'Stabilization Properties
    of Budgetary Systems: a Simulation Analysis' in Commission of the
    European Communities, 'The Economics of Community Public Finance',
    European Economy, Reports and Studies, 5.

Portes, R. (1993), 'EMS and EMU after the Fall', *The World Economy*, January.

Ravasio, G. (1994), 'The Progress of EMU in Everybody's Europe', speech at
    the Federal Trust Conference, 'EMU in a Multi-speed Europe', London,
    17 November.

Roll Committee (1993), *Independent and Accountable: A New Mandate for the
    Bank of England*, Report of an Independent Panel chaired by Eric Roll,
    London: Centre for Economic Policy Research, October.

Sachs, J. and X. Sala-i-Martin (1989), 'Fiscal Federalism and Optimum
    Currency Areas: Evidence for Europe from the United States', reprinted in
    M. Canzoneri, V. Grilli and P.R. Masson, eds, *Establishing a Central*

Bank: Issues in Europe and Lessons from the US, Cambridge: Cambridge University Press, 1992.

Santos, P. (1993), 'The Spatial Implications of Economic and Monetary Union', in Commission of the EC, 'The Economics of Public Finance', *European Economy*, Reports and Studies, 5.

Sardelis, C. (1993), *Targeting a European Monetary Aggregate*, EC Directorate-General for Economic and Financial Affairs, Economic Paper 102, July.

Schäuble, W. and K. Lamers (1994), 'Reflections on European Policy', CDU/CSU-Fraktion des Deutschen Bundestages, Bonn, September. Reprinted in K. Lamers, *A German Agenda for the European Union*, Federal Trust for Education and Research/Konrad Adenauer Foundation, 1994.

Schlesinger, H. (1993), *Challenges of European Integration: From the Single Market to the Monetary Union*, speech at the World Affairs Council, Los Angeles, 16 April.

Swinburne, M. and M. Castello-Branco (1991), *Central Bank Independence: Issues and Experience*, International Monetary Fund Working Paper, June.

Thygesen, N (1989), 'The Delors Report and European Economic and Monetary Union', *International Affairs*, Summer 1989.

Thygesen, N. (1993), *European Integration and the Single Currency*, paper for the Thirteenth Bank of France – University Conference on 'Capital Movements and Foreign Exchange Markets', Paris, 24–26 November.

Tietmeyer, H. (1994), *Europe on the Road to Monetary Integration*, speech at the German/Finnish Chamber of Commerce, Helsinki, 23 May.

Tietmeyer, H. (1995), *Experiences and Prospects for the Currency Union in Europe*, speech at the Friedrich Ebert Foundation, Hamburg, 30 January.

Treasury and Civil Service Select Committee (1993), *The Role of the Bank of England*, First Report, Vol. I, House of Commons Session 1993-4, London: HMSO, 8 December.

Turner, P. and J. Van't dack (1993), *Measuring International Price and Cost Competitiveness*, Bank for International Settlements Economic Papers, 39, November.

Tyrie, A. (1991), *A Cautionary Tale of EMU: Some Mistakes; Some Remedies*, Centre for Policy Studies, Policy Study, 121.

Ungerer, H., Hauvonen, J.J., Lopez-Claros, A. and T. Mayer (1990), *The European Monetary System: Developments and Prospects*, International Monetary Fund, Occasional Paper, 73.

Viñals, J. (1994), *Building a Monetary Union in Europe: Is it Worthwhile, Where do we Stand and Where are we Going?*, Centre for Economic Policy Research, Occasional Paper 15, October.

von Hagen, J. (1992), 'Fiscal Arrangements in a Monetary Union: Evidence from the US', in C. de Boissieu and D. Fair, eds, *Fiscal Policy, Taxes, and the Financial System in an Increasingly Integrated Europe*, Deventer: Kluwer.

References

Weber, A. A. (1991), 'EMU and Asymmetries and Adjustment Problems in the EMS – Some Empirical Evidence', in Commission of the European Communities 'The Economics of EMU', *European Economy*, Special Edition, 1.

Werner Report (1970), *Report to the Council and the Commission on the Realisation by Stages of Economic and Monetary Union in the Community*, Supplement to Bulletin II-1970 of the European Communities, Luxembourg.

Williamson, J. (1991), 'FEERs and the ERM', *National Institute Economic Review*, August.

Williamson, J. (1992), 'External Implications of EMU', in R. Barrell, ed., *Economic Convergence and Monetary Union in Europe*, Sage Publications for the NIESR.

Williamson, J. (1993a), 'Exchange Rate Management', *Economic Journal*, January.

Williamson, J. (1993b), 'EMS and EMU after the Fall: a Comment', *The World Economy*, May.

Williamson, J. (1993c), 'The Rise and fall of Political Support for EMU', in A. Giovannini, M. Guitian and R. Portes, eds, *The Monetary Future of Europe*, London: Centre for Economic Policy Research, Discussion Paper, March.

New Second Edition

THE BUNDESBANK
Germany's Central Bank in the International Monetary System

Ellen Kennedy

Reviews of the First Edition

'Essential reading for those who wish to understand the way the Bundesbank is organized, how it uses its powers, and the problems it faces in dealing with the German political authorities and with the uncertainties of the international system'

– International Affairs

'A first-rate study ... a particular strength is its analysis of how the Bundesbank functions as a largely independent entity within the German system'

– Foreign Affairs

The Bundesbank is crucial for the process of European monetary union and may provide the model for any future European Central Bank or 'Eurofed'. To understand the implications of this for the future of European monetary integration one must also understand the history and structure of the Bundesbank, its ethos and its objectives. This substantially revised and updated edition, incorporating material the author has gained from recent interviews with Bundesbank policy-makers, combines this historical perspective with a focus on the Bank's role both in German unification and in the movement towards monetary integration in Europe. It is a key study for anyone wanting to make sense of the new Europe.

Ellen Kennedy is Associate Professor of Political Science in the University of Pennsylvania. She has also taught at the Universities of Manchester, York and London and at the Albert-Ludwigs-Universität in Freiburg, where she was a fellow of the Alexander von Humboldt Foundation. She has written widely on German political culture and political theory.

144 pages; 216x138mm; ISBN 1 85567 315 0 (pbk)

December 1995 RIIA/Pinter Price £9.99